MW01686306

TIME TRACKS

Moments in History

Christine McClymont
James Barry
Berenice Wood

Published in 1994 simultaneously by:

Nelson Canada,
A Division of Thomson
Canada Limited
1120 Birchmount Road
Scarborough, Ontario
M1K 5G4
Canada

and

The Wright Group
19201 – 120th Avenue NE
Bothell, Washington
98011-9512
U.S.A.

ISBN 0-17-604367-5

1 2 3 4 5 /WC/ 97 96 95 94 93

ISBN 0-17-604399-3

1 2 3 4 5 /WC/ 97 96 95 94 93

I(T)P™
International Thomson Publishing
The trademark ITP is used under license

© Nelson Canada,
A Division of Thomson Canada Limited, 1994

All rights in this book are reserved.

As requested by individual copyright holders, some selections may retain original spellings, punctuation, usage, and style of measurement.

Project Manager: Lana Kong
Development: Susan Hughes
Assistant Editor: Carolyn Madonia
Senior Production Editor: Deborah Lonergan
Editorial Assistant: Camille Isaacs
Art Direction: Bruce Bond
Cover Design: Stuart Knox
Cover Photo: Bert Klassen

Printed and bound in Canada

Canadian Cataloguing in Publication Data

Main entry under title:
Time tracks : moments in history

(Nelson mini-anthologies)
ISBN 0-17-604367-5

1. Readers (Secondary). 2. World history – Juvenile literature. I. McClymont, Christine. II. Barry, James, 1939– . III. Wood, Berenice L. (Berenice Laura), 1947– . IV. Series.

PE1121.T54 1994 808′.0427 C93-095457-2

Series Review Panel

Lynn Archer, Language Arts Coordinator, Surrey School District No. 36, Surrey, B. C.
Sandie Bender, Academic Coordinator, Carleton Roman Catholic School Board, Nepean, Ont.
Mary Cahill, Resource Teacher, Winnipeg School Division No. 1, Winnipeg, Man.
Ross Elliott, Coordinator, English Program, Avalon North Integrated School Board, Spaniards Bay, Nfld.
Bob Ernest, English Consultant, Waterloo Board of Education, Waterloo, Ont.
Kathleen Gregory, Teacher, Sooke School District No. 62, Victoria, B. C.
Maureen Kennedy, Teacher, School District No. 17, Hillsborough, N. B.
Carole Kent, English Consultant, along with Teachers of the Halton Roman Catholic School Board, Burlington, Ont.
Regina Maher, Teacher, Saskatoon Roman Catholic Separate School Division No. 20, Saskatoon, Sask.
David Skeaff, Teacher, Northumberland and Newcastle Board of Education, Cobourg, Ont.
Mary Sullivan, Program Facilitator, Curriculum, County of Parkland No. 31, Stony Plain, Alta.
Carol Symons, Language Arts Consultant, Edmonton Public School Board, Edmonton, Alta.
Clevie Wall, Secondary Consultant, Dartmouth District School Board, Dartmouth, N. S.

Clem Marshall, Anti-Racist Consultant, MangaCom, Toronto, Ont.
Richard A. Murza, Teacher, Saskatoon Roman Catholic Separate School Division No. 20, Saskatoon, Sask. (History Consultant)

Dr. Dana Callen, Instructional Services for Leon County Schools, Tallahassee, FL
Dr. Michael F. Opitz, University of Southern Colorado, Pueblo, CO
Dr. Judith N. Thelen, Frostburg State University, Frostburg, MD

Table of Contents

B.C.E.: before the common era
C.E.: common era

I never realized that there was history, close at hand, beside my very own home. I did not realize that the old grave that stood among the brambles at the foot of our farm was history.

STEPHEN LEACOCK

THE FAR SIDE

by Gary Larson

"Oh, look, this get better ... 'F' in history! You even flunk something not happen yet!"

BELINDA ENRIQUEZ
PERIOD 3, ROOM 122

When I first came to history class
I sat in the last row, last seat
So I could read my romance novels
And not be bothered.
Some teachers notice what I'm reading; most don't,
But Miss Parsons did.
She didn't scream,
Or rip the book out of my hands,
Or toss it in the wastebasket.
She just whispered, "Quick, read these,
I've got a million of them—
Real life is better!"
And handed me a list of biographies of
Famous women in history.
I've read many of them—
Harriet Tubman, Joan of Arc, Susan B. Anthony.
I will always remember Miss Parsons's
Gentle smile and right words at the right time.
Maybe I should become a teacher.

Mel Glenn

WHEN DID HUMAN BEINGS BEGIN?

by Bruce Coville

Human beings live in the present and plan for the future. Perhaps even more importantly, we remember the past—and that's what history is all about.

"Where and when did human beings begin?"

This is a question about which scientists love to argue. To answer it, you first must answer another question: Just what *is* a human being?

Scientists once defined humans as "those animals that make and use tools." Then it was discovered that chimpanzees make simple tools.

Another distinction was that humans use language. Then we learned that chimps and gorillas can be taught simple forms of language.

While some people would like to give chimps and gorillas legal rights and protections, most are not willing to call these distant cousins humans. So the definition was revised again. Now scientists say, "Humans *habitually* make and use tools. They master *complex* language."

Some students of early humans would choose another kind of definition. Humans are self-aware. They do not live only in the present, but think of the future. They understand that someday they will die. They have the capacity to wonder. They do not simply accept the world as it is. Instead, they look at it and ask, "Why?"

So perhaps the beginning of the human species came in the moment when one of our ancient ancestors looked up at the sky and wondered why it had stars.

WHEELS MAKE THE WORLD GO ROUND

from Reader's Digest *Quest for the Past*

Historians disagree about who first used wheeled vehicles—the Mesopotamians or the Central Asians. But few people disagree that the wheel is the most important invention of all.

Of all the discoveries that have made human progress possible, none exceeds the wheel in importance. The invention of the wheel not only revolutionized transport but ushered in the age of machinery. Almost everything inside and outside the 20th-century home depends to some extent on the wheel. The motor in a washing machine is, in fact, just a sophisticated wheel, powered by the current generated by other wheels in electric turbines. Most modern textiles, from carpets to clothes, are made by machines that rely on the rotary principle. So are the pages of this book, and the letters you see printed on each page.

The wheel is so much the hub of our civilization that it is hard to believe that intelligent human beings could ever have managed without it. Yet for thousands of years after people first learned to grow crops and build cities, the wheel was unknown. And, curiously, despite its obvious usefulness for transport, the earliest known wheel was the potter's wheel, which was probably invented in Mesopotamia about 5500 years ago.

The first potter's wheels were flat discs, usually of stone or wood, with a central hollow on the underside that fitted over a stone or hardwood dome set in the ground. At first these were simply turntables, useful only for bringing different sections of the pot within easy reach of the potter, but the technique of forming pots on a constantly spinning wheel soon followed. Part of one such wheel, made of clay, has been found at the ancient Mesopotamian city of Ur (possible birthplace of Abraham). Dating from about 3250 B.C.E., it has a series of holes around the circumference. The holes would have made it easier for the potter to grip the wheel when he or she set it spinning.

Archeologists have been able to trace the evolution of the potter's wheel in some detail by studying the telltale finger grooves and the direction of the particles in the clay walls of wheel-thrown pots. When and where the principle of the wheel was first applied to transport remains unknown, however, since very few examples of early wheeled vehicles have survived. It is generally agreed that the first wheeled vehicle was probably a four-wheeled cart, which must have come into use shortly after the invention of the potter's wheel.

Scholars have suggested two regions as possible sources of this revolutionary device: the city-states of Mesopotamia or the steppes of Central Asia. Most of the available evidence points to Mesopotamia as the likely place, but some scholars argue that no evidence has been found on the steppes only because the nomads who lived there built no cities for modern-day archeologists to explore. In support of this argument they point out that the flat, open land of the Asian steppes was more suited to wheeled transport than the soft sand of Mesopotamia. Moreover the Mesopotamian cities moved most of their freight by river—a far more efficient method of transport in the roadless conditions of the time—and so had no pressing need to invent the wheeled vehicle though they must have been quick to perceive its advantages once it came along.

Although the claims for both regions as inventor of the wheel remain tantalizingly plausible, most archeologists believe that the wheel was invented only once, not in several places independently. They base this conviction on the remarkable uniformity of design among ancient carts that have been discovered in places as far apart as Western Europe, Egypt, India, and China. Almost all have two important—and not obvious—features in common: a shaft designed for yoking two animals and a spokeless wheel made up of three distinct pieces of wood held together by cross-struts. Had wheeled vehicles been invented in more than one region, the experts say, there would surely be differences in the way they were pulled and the construction of the wheels.

At first the carts were usually drawn by oxen, just as ploughs had been for thousands of years, and they were used mostly to move goods over short distances—from a farm to a nearby market, say—or to carry dignitaries in ceremonial processions. But two later developments turned these relatively clumsy and largely agricultural vehicles into the world's first war machines. The two developments, which appeared more or less simultaneously in about 2000 B.C.E., were the taming of horses and the development of the spoked wheel. The result was a light, fast chariot that could outrun even the best infantry.

Whatever its origin, the new invention brought dramatic changes in its wake as it spread across the ancient world, reaching Western Europe by 1550 B.C.E. and eastern China by 1300. The mere existence of efficient wheeled vehicles created a need for a network of better roads; better roads speeded up the development of trade; and traders, administrators, and armies could travel farther and faster than ever before, making it possible for aggressive peoples to conquer ever-larger territories. Archeologists have argued that without the spoked wheel, it is probable that the Hittite warriors from Central Asia could never have conquered the Anatolian plateau of central Turkey as they did in about 1850 B.C.E., the Assyrians could not have brought all mainland Greece under their control, and the Shang dynasty could not have founded the first major Chinese empire.

By permission of Johnny Hart and Creators Syndicate, Inc.

THE EGYPTIANS PREPARE FOR LIFE AFTER DEATH

by Catherine Chadefaud

Ancient Egypt is one of the most famous early civilizations, thanks to discoveries like King Tut's tomb, but most of all to the pyramids—still standing after more than 4000 years.

Houses of Eternity

On the edge of the Libyan Desert, the pyramids overhang the Nile Valley. Every morning at dawn they emerge from the mist rising from the river, ghostly shapes seeming to float above the palm trees, vast monuments which have fascinated travellers of every age. During the Islamic middle ages, they were identified as the granaries that Joseph, in the Bible story, built in preparation for the seven years of famine. Some people believed they concealed the pharaoh's wealth; one sultan even tried to open up the pyramid of Khufu to get at its treasure. Yet others have seen them as a centre of cryptic culture, keys to the secret of the meaning of life. People have taken their measurements in order to discover the golden number on which their construction was based.

Most of the pyramids were built between the Third and the Sixth Dynasties (2780–2280 B.C.E.). Some were still being built during the Middle Kingdom (about 2050–1800 B.C.E.) after a long period of troubles. Their shapes and the methods used to construct them changed as the centuries went by. The oldest was built for King Djoser, in the Third Dynasty. His architect, the scribe Imhotep, built the first great stone pyramid, now known as the Step Pyramid. The pyramid is made of a series of six *mastabas* (Arabic for "bench"), shallow rectangular tombs, one on top of the other. Later, under the Fourth Dynasty rulers Khufu, Khafra, and Menkure, pyramids with triangular sides rising to a peak rose up on the plain of Giza.

How these gigantic monuments were built still remains something of a mystery. It is known that local peasants and artisans were drafted to take part in the building, by a kind of forced labour system. Very early on, several organizations tried to free themselves from this obligation, and tables were drawn up exempting certain workers.

Pyramids were built by the ancient Egyptians as royal tombs, in preparation for their rulers' deaths. They were always part of an architectural complex. This complex included a lower temple in the valley, marking the entrance to the area and linked by a ramp to an upper temple where ritual offerings were made after the pharaoh's death. This sanctuary sprang to life after the royal funeral when the pyramid was finally sealed.

These great tombs give little indication of the life of the ruler after his death. Only the most recent, from the Fifth and Seventh Dynasties, contain instructions written on the inside walls, in the corridors down to the tomb and in the burial vault. These "Pyramid Texts," as they are known, were magical and religious formulas for protecting the king on his passage through the world of the gods. Like a divine falcon, the pharaoh would take flight. Then he would board the boat of Re, the god of the sun, which renewed life every day for all eternity. The civil servants hoped that the king's immortality would rub off on them, and so they built their own tombs close by. Thus were born huge necropolises, or cemeteries. These Cities of the Dead, as they were known, reverberated with the sounds of the living who were appointed to look after them.

A Religion of Eternal Life

When someone died, the family would carry the body to the sector where the embalmers lived and worked. There they would leave it for 40 to 70 days, to go through the long process of mummification before burial. First the embalmers would remove the inner organs and place them in separate urns; then they would treat the body and organs in dry natron (a salt compound) to dry them out. The body was then laid on a huge alabaster table and wrapped in fine linen bandages, into which were inserted protective amulets[1] provided by the family.

The ritual embalmer then placed between the mummy's legs a papyrus roll. This roll, now called "The Book of the Dead," contained some good sayings about the deceased intended to help in the next life. This kind of preparation was very expensive, and the poor could aspire to no more than a coarse woven wrapping with a few amulets and burial in the desert sand.

Life after death was a major concern of the Egyptians, and it could only be guaranteed if the body was preserved as an imperishable container for the soul. Thus only the great were able to travel in Re's underground boat and accompany Osiris, god of vegetation and rebirth. Even then, those who desired eternal life had numerous obstacles to overcome. Demons, armed with knives, lay in wait for them. They had to pass through bolted doors and cross a mysterious labyrinth full of caverns. According to some traditions, a dead person who passed all these tests could enjoy eternal peace in the "Fields of Reeds," the paradise of the just. But the outcome of the journey depended on the judgement of Osiris, who weighed the heart, the seat of the soul, in the Hall of Double Justice. The name of the dead person was written on the coffin and the tomb as a symbol and guarantee of continued survival. For the Egyptians, giving something a name meant giving it life. To remove or mutilate someone's name brought eternal death. This is why people removed their enemies' names from monuments.

At birth, the name given to a child placed it under the protection of a particular god. Ptahmose meant "he who is born of Pteh"; Amenhotep meant "Ammon is satisfied"; Mutnedjmet meant "the goddess Mut is pleased." A name was thus a privilege, a link that united a person with the gods in life and at death became an indispensable guarantee of immortality.

1. **amulet:** An object worn to protect against evil.

THE GREEKS EXPLORE IDEAS

by Sophia A. Boyer and Winifred Lubell

The civilization of ancient Greece lasted from about 2000 to 200 B.C.E. Between 500 and 400 B.C.E., the city-state of Athens became famous for its artists, its politicians, and its philosophers (literally, lovers of wisdom). Greek philosophers questioned common beliefs in order to find new ideas and explore new truths.

Socrates, Plato, and Aristotle were the greatest philosophers of the ancient world, and no other Greeks have made such an impact on later ages. They concerned themselves with the same questions that philosophers have explored ever since. What is the purpose of the world? What is a good person? Does a good society make good people, or good people a good society?

Philosophers of the present day pursue these questions in classrooms, libraries, and studies full of books and papers. The Greek philosophers pursued the same problems in gymnasiums. A Greek "gymnasium" was a large tract of land containing groves of trees, gardens full of statues, colonnaded walks, and sometimes small theatres, as well as racetracks, stadiums, and public baths. There the philosophers walked and talked with their students and associates.

Socrates spent all of the daylight hours of his adult life either in a gymnasium or on the streets of Athens and the *agora* (marketplace). In the evening he often continued to talk at a friend's house, sometimes till dawn of the following day. He was a familiar sight to all Athenians, a short man with a big belly, a small button nose, and a gait described as a waddle. He scorned money and worldly possessions. Socrates's method of pursuing philosophy was to ask questions. His seemingly simple and innocent questions trapped his pupils into examining their beliefs. He turned philosophy toward ethics, the study of human behaviour. Socrates lived in the great days of Athenian democracy and on into the beginning of its decline. He was particularly concerned with the *polis* (city-state), and he frequently discussed with his pupil Plato what made a perfect state.

Socrates, about 40 years older than Plato, was 70 in 399 B.C.E., the year of his death. He had lived into the period of the war between Athens and Sparta and the time of a plague that wiped out much of the Athenian population. Perhaps these events contributed to the growing mood of suspicion and fear of new philosophies—a mood unusual in Athens, where respect for freedom of speech and thought had been the rule. In any case, Socrates was accused of corrupting the young by teaching them of new divinities, and he was condemned to die by drinking a cup of hemlock, a poisonous drink.

No one mourned for Socrates more than his devoted follower Plato. But the two men had often disagreed, and the philosophy taught by Plato was very different from that of his master. It, too, was concerned with human conduct, but Plato scorned the democratic *polis* that Socrates admired. Plato wrote about an ideal state that would be run by the few best-educated and most intelligent men. One of his best-known theories was that there is a world of the mind, of ideas, superior to that of the physical world.

Plato wrote his books in the form of dialogues or conversations, with Socrates as the principal character. It is from Plato alone that we know what Socrates taught, for he himself wrote down nothing.

Aristotle, who lived from 384 to 322 B.C.E., was a pupil of Plato. Most of his life was spent at Athens, but it was a very different Athens from that which Plato and Socrates had known, and before Aristotle's death it was under the rule of Macedon. Aristotle studied with Plato when he was young, and then went to Macedon to be a tutor to young Alexander. Later he returned to Athens and taught philosophy. He taught ethics and politics like his two great predecessors, but he also made important contributions in subjects they never touched. Aristotle did work that laid the foundation for several major sciences. He inaugurated a truly scientific method of study, making observations of plants and animals and carefully recording his findings. He was able to carry on this work on a large scale with the help of between 400 and 1000 students, aided by money from Alexander the Great (his former student). This scientific work that Aristotle directed marked the beginnings of zoology, biology, and botany.

The influence of the Greek philosophers is hard to exaggerate. Their ideas dominated the Aegean and Near Eastern world at the time that Christianity was taking shape and had a profound influence on Christian doctrine. (The New Testament was written in Greek.) During the Middle Ages, Aristotle was greatly admired, but in more recent times, many have considered Plato the master philosopher. Alfred North Whitehead, a 20th-century English philosopher, said that all European philosophy consists of "footnotes" on Plato.

This was the end of our friend; a man of whom we may say that of all whom we met at that time he was the wisest and justest and best.

PLATO, WRITING ABOUT THE DEATH OF SOCRATES

HANNIBAL CROSSES THE ALPS WITH ELEPHANTS

from Reader's Digest *Quest for the Past*

The mighty Roman Empire was at war with Carthage (near modern-day Tunis on the North African coast) for control of the western Mediterranean. In 218 B.C.E., Hannibal, a Carthaginian commander, decided to invade Italy by a surprise route—straight through the mountains. He was amazingly successful, managing to hold the Romans at bay for 15 years. The Punic Wars finally ended, however, with Hannibal's suicide and the destruction of Carthage.

To the desert-bred North Africans of the Carthaginian army the mountains looked formidable. Austere and aloof, they rose up so sharply that their summits vanished into the clouds. Confronted with a swirling grey world of echoing mountain passes (and probably hostile gods), the shivering soldiers longed for a return to the warm plains they had left behind.

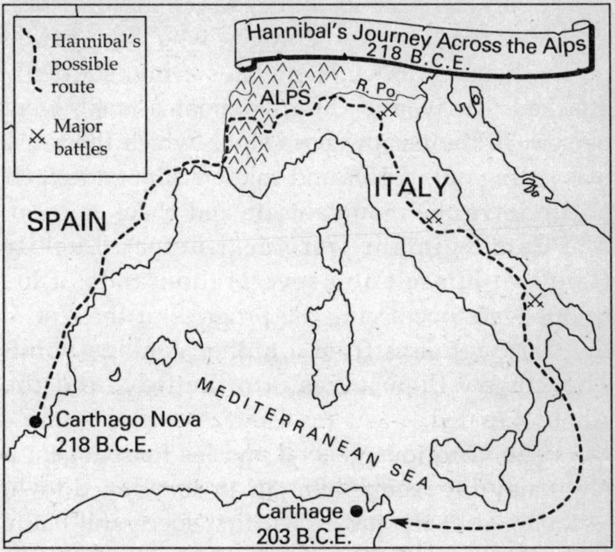

For Hannibal, their commander, the decision to lead an army of 40 000 troops, several thousand horses, and 40 elephants across the Alps was the most momentous of his military career. Still only 29, he had been commander-in-chief of Carthaginian forces for three years and had a reputation for audacity second to none. He knew that the Roman enemy, expecting him to invade Italy from the north along the coastal route, had placed an army there to stop him. That was why, in the fall of 218 b.c.e., he decided to go over the Alps even though the feat of taking a large force up and over this rocky and in some places ice-covered terrain had never before been attempted.

Soon after the army began its climb, tribespeople of the hostile Allobroges, who were poised on the heights above Hannibal's army, suddenly attacked. The wounded Carthaginian animals went berserk in the narrow pass along which the army was strung out; horses and soldiers slipped to their death down the mountainside and chaos reigned. The Carthaginians were near defeat. Luckily Hannibal himself and several thousands of his troops were overseeing the progress of the rest of the Carthaginians from a higher vantage point. They threw themselves into the fray, and the Allobroges fled.

The victorious general and his forces spent a night and day recuperating in an abandoned town at the head of the pass. That first successful battle in the Alps won them a short breathing space, thus enabling the army to make considerable progress. Some days later, local tribespeople eager for loot offered to provide guides to help Hannibal find a way through the mountains. The guides took the army through a deep gorge that had a cliff rising above one side of the track, a precipice on the other, and a number of the fellow-tribespeople, armed with rocks, at the top of the cliffs.

There was no way the Carthaginians could avoid the onslaught. Boulders crashed down all along the column, causing appalling loss of life; and this time the panic was not confined to the animals. The Carthaginian column was cut in two, and Hannibal and some of the soldiers were forced to spend the night on a large rock formation warding off continual attacks, while the remainder of the army struggled through the darkness.

Hannibal rejoined the rest of his troops the next morning. For a few days the tribespeople continued to harass the Carthaginians, but they were apparently too frightened of the elephants to attack the army directly, and so they withdrew. But now the terrain was changing, becoming more menacing than the worst of human enemies. At the highest point of the crossing, Carthaginian morale nearly evaporated. The slopes all around were covered with ice; there was no grazing for livestock, no shelter, no respite. Without reliable guides, the army often took wrong turnings, forcing the cumbersome baggage train to retrace its steps again and again. The soldiers felt increasingly trapped and defeated. Of the 40 000 troops who went into the Alps with Hannibal, it is estimated that fewer than 14 000 survived to reach the other side.

On the 10th day of the crossing, with the army at its last gasp, the outlook suddenly changed. For 10 days the soldiers had seen nothing but immense, seemingly impassable mountains in front of them. Now, all of a sudden, they caught a glimpse of their goal: Italy. There, stretched out far below, were the plains of the River Po, warm and inviting in the sunshine. For two days the soldiers camped overlooking the Po to recover their strength and allow stragglers to catch up. They then began a descent that took three days and cost more lives. It is a measure of Hannibal's stature as a general that, by the time they reached the bottom of the treacherous slopes, they were once again a disciplined body of soliders as they poured onto the Italian plain. It was the Romans who had confidently declared war against far-away Carthage. Now Hannibal had done the unthinkable and carried the battle into Roman territory.

Historians still argue about which of several different passes over the Alps the Carthaginians chose to follow; there is no argument about the extent of their achievement.

Time Capsule
WOMEN MAKE THEIR MARK

These four women achieved great power, and changed the course of history in their countries.

Trung Trac and Trung Nhi, ruled parts of Vietnam, 40–43 C.E.

by Jessica Amanda Salmonson

Enraged by the atrocities of a Chinese governor who had executed her husband, Trung Trac began to organize a Vietnamese peasant revolt. She wrote her proclamation of revolution upon the skin of a previously invincible tiger that had terrorized villagers, which she had slain as evidence of her might. She was an even greater military tactician than tiger slayer; nevertheless, it was her sister, Trung Nhi, who became the more famous in battle. Together in 40 C.E., these sisters led an army of 80 000 against the tyrant To Dinh, who shaved his head and beard to flee to China as a monk. It was the first time in 1000 years that Vietnam had been free of Chinese dominion.

The Trungs took control of 65 fortified towns

and continued for three years to threaten the Chinese government in Vietnam. Thirty-six lesser generals, all women, were selected and trained by the famed sisters, including the Trungs' own mother. When Chinese reinforcements defeated the tactically superior Trungs by weight of numbers alone, the women escaped capture by performing suicide in its most dignified, heroic context, centuries before the Japanese had codified the procedure of hara-kiri.

In the centuries to follow, the Trungs became idealized examples of national courage. They were deified; temples were built to their honour in the 12th century, at least one of which still stands in Hanoi, where the anniversary of their suicide is a recognized holiday. In the 18th century, a nationalist movement selected a native emperor who gave the two Trung generals posthumous titles of nobility as a direct counter to Chinese/Confucian attempts to belittle the Trungs' ancient exploits.

"Trung" has become the Vietnamese word for "Amazon," connoting patriotic valour.

Jingo Kogo, ruled Japan for 70 years during the second century C.E.

by Jessica Amanda Salmonson

A martial empress of Japan, skilled with sword and bow, Jingo Kogo (also called Okinaga Tarashi) conquered Korea in 201 C.E. She instructed her navy, "Do not rape or plunder. Do not fear many or despise few. Give mercy to all who yield but no quarter to the stubborn. Victors will be rewarded; deserters will be slain." Among the tributes she brought back to Japan was her nation's first written language.

Jingo Kogo governed for 70 years. She was succeeded by her son Emperor Ojin, deified after his death as the War-god Hachiman; hence Jingo Kogo is considered the Mother of War.

Elizabeth I, ruled England 1558–1603

by Kenneth and Valerie McLeish

Elizabeth was the youngest surviving child of King Henry VIII. During the reign of Mary, her elder sister, England was brought to the edge of financial and political ruin. This was partly because of wars against the French and partly because of fighting in England itself, between Protestants and Catholics.

In 1558, when Elizabeth succeeded her older sister Mary as Queen, she quickly made peace with France. But she refused to keep England Catholic, as it had been under Mary. This angered the Catholic kings of Spain. The Spaniards were also angered by the way Elizabeth refused to punish Sir Walter Raleigh, Sir Francis Drake, and other English sea captains for attacking Spanish ships and settlements in the New World. Finally in 1588, King Philip II of Spain sent a huge *armada* (armed fleet) to attack Britain. Some of the ships were destroyed by the British. Some were blown off-course by storms and sunk. The armada was no longer a threat, although the war between Spain and England dragged on for years.

Elizabeth never married. Her long reign restored the prosperity England had lost in Mary's time and gave it back the glory it had known under Henry VIII. Queen Elizabeth favoured writers and musicians and encouraged explorers and adventurers. British people still look back on her reign, the time of writers such as William Shakespeare, as one of the most glittering periods of their history.

Catherine II ("The Great"), ruled Russia 1762–1796

from **Great Lives**

Catherine the Great was Empress of Russia from 1762 until her death. She was an ambitious, calculating daughter of a Prince of Prussia, who saw that marriage (in 1745) to the future Tsar Peter III could make her powerful. Catherine hated her husband, who was a weak man, and they soon became enemies. Six months after Peter became Tsar in 1762 he was deposed and then murdered by two of Catherine's lovers, Count Grigory Orlov and Prince Grigory Potemkin. Catherine immediately declared herself empress, although her son was in fact next in line to the throne.

Catherine was an energetic and effective ruler. Wars with Turkey (in 1774 and 1792) and with Sweden (in 1790) increased the size of her empire, and when Poland was divided up, Russia gained all of the area known as the Ukraine. Catherine abolished capital punishment for everything except political crimes and planned to introduce a new education system and legal reforms. These last changes were never effective, and for many poor Russians life became worse under Catherine because there were more soldiers needed and therefore more taxes to pay. Her government was threatened by a revolt in 1773, led by a man who claimed he was Catherine's dead husband. Meanwhile, life in the royal court was extravagant and full of minor intrigues. Catherine herself recorded the events of her reign in her *Memoirs*.

VESUVIUS ERUPTS, DESTROYING POMPEII

by Catherine George

Pompeii, a prosperous Italian city in the Roman Empire, vanished in one of history's greatest tragedies—and lay buried for more than 17 centuries.

By all accounts August 24, 79 C.E. began as an idyllic summer's day. The morning sun shone warmly on the prosperous cosmopolitan city at the southern flank of Mount Vesuvius.

If there had been any hint of the catastrophic events that were to follow, citizens had paid no heed. Only the animals seemed to sense the turmoil that was taking place within the earth that day. Dogs howled at some unseen force and sheep and cattle had been unusually restless.

Merchants, importers, and artisans conducted their trades in shops and market stalls along the Via dell'Abbondanza, the main shopping street. Women and slaves went about domestic duties while children played in courtyard gardens, unaware of the seething monster concealed within the bowels of the mountain.

Around the forum, in the city centre, businesspeople and bankers had gathered to discuss politics, religion, and economic matters. Actors were rehearsing at the two elaborate theatres, and gladiators had been preparing for evening games at the 20 000-seat amphitheatre.

Those occupied with matters of less worldly importance were escaping the midday sun at more than 100 taverns and cafés scattered throughout Pompeii. Others were relaxing and socializing at the three public baths.

Masons and carpenters were busy rebuilding several of the temples and the imposing basilica destroyed in a devastating earthquake 17 years earlier (Pompeiians didn't interpret that quake as a portent of the tragedy that was to come).

Outside the city walls, wealthy landowners and nobles from Rome had been relaxing in their luxurious mountainside villas with unobstructed views across the azure waters of the Bay of Naples, all the way to the sunwashed isles of Capri and Ischia. Gentle breezes off the Tyrrhenian Sea stirred the perfumes of hibiscus, rose, and almond as slaves tended to olive orchards and flourishing vineyards on the mountain slopes. Few were aware that beneath them Vesuvius was a brooding volcano.

For the 5000 residents of the equally prosperous fishing port and upper-class resort of

Herculaneum, 16 km to the northwest, the day had been progressing much the same way.

The end came. Abrupt and terrifying.

Vesuvius Erupts

Without warning Vesuvius awakened from its thousand-year sleep and with all the might of an atomic bomb, the pent-up monster hidden beneath the floor of its crater exploded in a violent and fiery rage.

Red-hot lava, earth, and stone shot 32 km into the sky, forming a black cloud that blotted out the sun. Cinders, pumice, and wet ash rained down, enveloping the earth in total blackness. Birds dropped dead from the sky.

In the space of a few terrible hours, a fleeting instant in the span of time, Pompeii and Herculaneum passed from existence, and all forms of life around them were extinguished from the face of the earth.

The majority of Pompeii's estimated 20 000 citizens fled to the safety of the sea in the early hours of the eruption. Others had noticed the innocuous film of ash and had sensed tremors in the earth earlier in the month and, recalling the disastrous quake of 62 C.E., had moved to safer ground. But at least 2000 of Pompeii's population had elected to stay.

Those who remained sought refuge in their homes and public buildings but were either trapped or crushed when roofs and walls collapsed from the weight of falling rock. Some panicked, attempting to flee, but in the blackness they lost their way and died in agony trying to shield themselves from the violence from above. Pompeii had become a hell from which there was no escape.

Debris plummetted from the sky covering a 10-km radius around Vesuvius and retiring the Bay of Naples for five kilometres. In subsequent writings Pliny the Younger, who had witnessed the apocalypse descending upon the city, truly believed that it was the end of the world and described what he saw as "an eternal night come upon the world."

The eruptions continued for three days and three nights.

In its final paroxysm, Vesuvius set off electrical storms causing fires, earthquakes, and tidal waves as it continued to spew avalanches of red-hot ashes, lava, and lethal gases down its slopes, asphyxiating all remaining life. (It was not a sea of flaming lava, but falling rock and poison gases that killed most of the victims.)

1750 Years of Silence

When the volcano finally silenced itself, Pompeii lay buried beneath seven metres of pumice and ash and Herculaneum had drowned in 20 m of debris. When the cinders had cooled, some of the population returned to claim personal belongings and to loot the treasures near the surface. But for most, Pompeii had become a feared place, under an evil spell, a city of the dead, cursed by the gods.

The wet ash and lava quickly solidified, sealing both cities and protecting them from the ravages of time. And so they remained, silent and hidden, all but forgotten, for more than 1750 years. There were six major eruptions throughout the following centuries (one in 1631 may have killed 18 000 people) entombing the cities even deeper.

It wasn't until 1860, under a united Italy, that Victor Emmanuel II appointed archeologist Giuseppe Fiorelli to do a systemized and orderly excavation of Pompeii. It was under Fiorelli's guidance that one of history's great tragedies came to light as one of archeology's great discoveries.

Three-quarters of the 66-ha city has been excavated and the remains speak with clarity of the life of the classical Romans, a civilization not unlike our own. Though they worshipped various gods, they had a system of moral laws on which today's democratic society is based.

Pompeii Today

As you walk about Pompeii you'll notice its four main streets are paved with white volcanic stone making it easier to see at night. Avenues were built on slopes with pedestrian stepping stones and gutters for drainage. Ruts carved by cart and chariot wheels 2000 years ago are plainly visible.

Beneath the streets lead pipes carried water from aqueducts to fountains, baths, and courtyard pools. (Lead poisoning from water pipes and cooking pots may have contributed to the demise of the Roman Empire according to some historians.)

Public baths and saunas had double walls with sophisticated heating systems between. Slaves stoked wood furnaces to keep heat circulating. Visit the Stabian baths and you'll see a Roman-style fitness centre complete with lockers, hot and cold baths and saunas, an exercise yard, and massage chamber.

Living accommodation ranged from small apartments to large multi-storey houses. Most dwellings were designed without windows to keep out heat and humidity. Murals with outdoor scenes were painted on walls to create the feeling of space; light came from roof openings and shaded courtyards.

The huge columned forum was the heart of Pompeii life. It was a place to gossip and market, it was where municipal affairs and religious services took place, and the law courts and more than 40 statues to the gods were located there including the temples of Apollo and Jupiter. Citizens spent evenings in the huge amphitheatre watching gladiators battle each other and at times bears, lions, and other wild animals.

Graffiti was prevalent in Roman times. More than 6000 inscriptions have been uncovered on exterior walls, messages that speak of love, politics, pleas, curses, predictions. "Nothing in the world can endure forever" is one of the more memorable etchings by an ancient philosopher.

Archeological findings tell us that the Romans ate well. Remains of agricultural produce, meat, and food from the sea was found on display in shops and groceries, and food was found in cooking pots and urns, as if those preparing it had left with every intention of returning. Bread was discovered in bakery ovens reminding us of how suddenly life had stopped.

The Volcano's Victims

But the most wrenching and poignant sight in all of Pompeii is the remains of its suffocated victims. It's all there in their facial expressions, the agony and horror they experienced in the last throes of death 19 centuries ago.

The powdery volcanic ash, moistened by the rain, had molded to the contours of the victims' bodies and hardened. Once the flesh decayed it left the skeleton encased in a cavity that archaeologists were able to fill with liquid plaster. The plaster solidified so successfully that we are able to see facial expressions, even the folds of the victims' clothing.

Casts have immortalized hundreds of victims of the disaster. They speak to us from the past—contorted figures with outstretched arms shielding children; prisoners in chains pleading for release; a family of eight fleeing toward the safety of the sea. Casts were taken of animals trapped with their masters; dogs struggled at the ends of tethers and a mule trying to charge its stable door was found with its head stuck partway through.

Today, a new Pompeii, Campo Pompeiano, has sprung up around the ancient ruins. The volcano, looming in the background, last erupted in 1944, blowing its entire centre away. In 1980 a damaging earthquake forced the closing of parts of the excavated city.

Although it has been relatively quiet for half a century, Mount Vesuvius occasionally makes its presence known with a rumble and a belch of smoke—a flagrant reminder that the monster within has yet to be subdued.

Pliny the Younger lived in Italy during the time of the Roman Empire. He was only 17 when he witnessed and described the most famous eruption in history:

Soon afterwards the cloud sank down to earth and covered the sea; it had already blotted out Capri and hidden the promontory Misenum from sight. Then my mother implored, entreated, and commanded me to escape as best I could—a young man might escape, whereas she was old and slow and could die in peace as long as she had not been the cause of my death too. I refused to save myself without her, and grasping her hand forced her to quicken her pace. She gave in reluctantly, blaming herself for delaying me.

Ashes were already falling, not as yet very thickly. I looked round: a dense black cloud was coming up behind us, spreading over the earth like a flood.

"Let us leave the road while we can still see," I said, "or we shall be knocked down and trampled underfoot in the dark by the crowd behind."

We had scarcely sat down to rest when darkness fell, not the dark of a moonless or cloudy night, but as if the lamp had been put out in a closed room. You could hear the shrieks of women, the wailing of infants, and the shouting of men; some were calling their parents, others their children or their wives, trying to recognize them by their voices. People bewailed their own fate or that of their relatives, and there were some who prayed for death in their terror of dying. Many besought the aid of the gods, but still more imagined there were no gods left, and that the universe was plunged into eternal darkness for evermore. There were people, too, who added to the real perils by inventing fictitious dangers: some reported that part of Misenum had collapsed or another part was on fire, and though their tales were false they found others to believe them.

A gleam of light returned, but we took this to be a warning of the approaching flames rather than daylight. However, the flames remained some distance off; then darkness came on once more and ashes began to fall again, this time in heavy showers. We rose from time to time and shook them off, otherwise we should have been buried and crushed beneath their weight. I could boast that not a groan or cry of fear escaped me in these perils, but I admit that I derived some poor consolation in my mortal lot from the belief that the whole world was dying with me and I with it.

THE VIKINGS SAIL TO NEWFOUNDLAND

by Suzanne LeVert

For centuries, people believed Christopher Columbus was the first European to lay eyes on the New World. But we now know that long before Columbus, intrepid sailors from Norway had crossed the wild Atlantic Ocean.

In 1961, a team of Norwegian archeologists made one of the most important discoveries in Newfoundland's history: They found the remains of an ancient Viking settlement at l'Anse aux Meadows on the northern peninsula of the island. The findings confirmed that Norse adventurers had found their way across the Atlantic to Newfoundland as early as 1000 C.E. They are now thought to have been the first Europeans ever to see North America.

Norse legends recount that centuries ago certain Vikings sailed from the Norse colonies in Iceland and Greenland to lands farther west. One saga told of Bjarni Herjolfsson, a Viking who was blown off course while sailing from Iceland to Greenland in about 985 C.E. When he finally arrived in Greenland, he spoke of three new lands he had seen in the west. One was forested and hilly, another was forested and flat, and the third was rocky and mountainous. Scholars believe that Herjolfsson had sighted the coasts of Newfoundland, Labrador, and Baffin Island.

Leif Eriksson was one of the Vikings in Greenland who heard Herjolfsson's story. A dozen years later, Eriksson bought Herjolfsson's ship and went in search of the western lands that Herjolfsson had described. Eriksson and his men landed in three places, which they called Helluland (Rocky Land), Markland (Wooded Land), and Vinland (Wine Land, meaning that it had fruit). Historians now believe that these three landings correspond to the east coast of Labrador, the northern coast of Newfoundland island, and a warm, sheltered bay either on the southern coast of Newfoundland or on Cape Breton Island, Nova Scotia. The Vikings spent the winter in Vinland and returned to Greenland the following spring.

Later, other Norse expeditions visited the new western territory. A few settlements were established in Vinland, including the l'Anse aux Meadows site in Newfoundland, but the settlements were abandoned after attacks by the local Natives, whom the Norse called *skraellings*. The Norse colony in Greenland died out in the 14th century, and knowledge of Vinland and other areas that the Vikings had visited in North America was limited to sagas and legends.

The Natives

The Vikings did not find an uninhabited new world. A variety of Native people had lived in Labrador and on Newfoundland island for centuries. A tribe who called themselves the Mushuau Innu (Barren Land People) lived in central Labrador and northern Newfoundland. Referred to as the Montagnais-Naskapi by Europeans, these Natives were nomadic hunters of caribou and other mammals. They were adept at travelling across their expansive hunting grounds, using canoes during the summer and snowshoes and toboggans during the winter. When the Europeans came to the region in the 15th and 16th centuries, the Innu helped them to start the fur trade that would eventually spread into most of present-day Canada.

North of the Innu lived the Inuit, who were called Eskimos by the southern tribes. The Inuit lived in small communities scattered throughout the Arctic from Alaska to Greenland, including northern Labrador. They were hunters and gatherers who moved seasonally from one camp to another. They spoke a language known as Inuktitut, which is still spoken by many of the more than 25 000 Inuit who live in Canada today.

The Dorset were another Native people living in Newfoundland at the time of the Viking expeditions. Descended from an ancient Arctic culture, the Dorset lived on Newfoundland island from about 500 B.C.E. until about 1500 C.E. Distantly related to the Inuit, the Dorset lived in houses built of snow and turf. They hunted sea mammals such as the walrus and the narwhal, an Arctic whale.

The interior and the southern coast of Newfoundland were inhabited by the Micmac. This Native group lived in villages all along the east coast of North America, from Massachusetts to Quebec. The Micmac outnumbered the other Native peoples in Newfoundland, and they helped the European settlers survive their first hard winters in the New World. Several thousand Micmac still live in Newfoundland; other Micmac live throughout Atlantic Canada.

The Beothuk people lived on the southern and northeastern coasts of the island. They may well have been the first Natives encountered by Europeans in North America; historians now believe that the *skraellings* who fought with the Vikings were either Beothuk or Dorset fishermen. The Beothuk painted their faces with red dye for certain ceremonies, and some scholars have suggested that *redskin*, a term once used for Native people, may have referred to this custom. The Beothuk lived in tents covered with bark or animal skin, and they used bows and arrows for hunting and harpoons for fishing. They numbered about 2000 when English and French settlers began arriving in the 17th and 18th centuries.

MARCO POLO MEETS THE GREAT KUBLAI KHAN

by Kim Dramer

Lucky Marco Polo! The boy from Venice was only 17 when he accompanied his uncle and father on a journey to the fabulous kingdom of China, ruled by the great Kublai Khan. When he returned to Venice in 1295, it is said that his relatives didn't recognize him—and no wonder. Polo had been travelling, almost continually, for 25 years. Luckily for us, Marco later wrote a book describing his experiences.

In the middle of the 13th century, trade along the Silk Route began to flourish again. This fragile line of overland trading routes, stretching from China through the oases of central Asia, the towns and marketplaces of Persia, and finally to the ports of the eastern Mediterranean, had been closed to European merchants for hundreds of years by hostile Muslim governments. To the people of the West, China was a great mystery and Japan completely unknown. But with the conquests of the

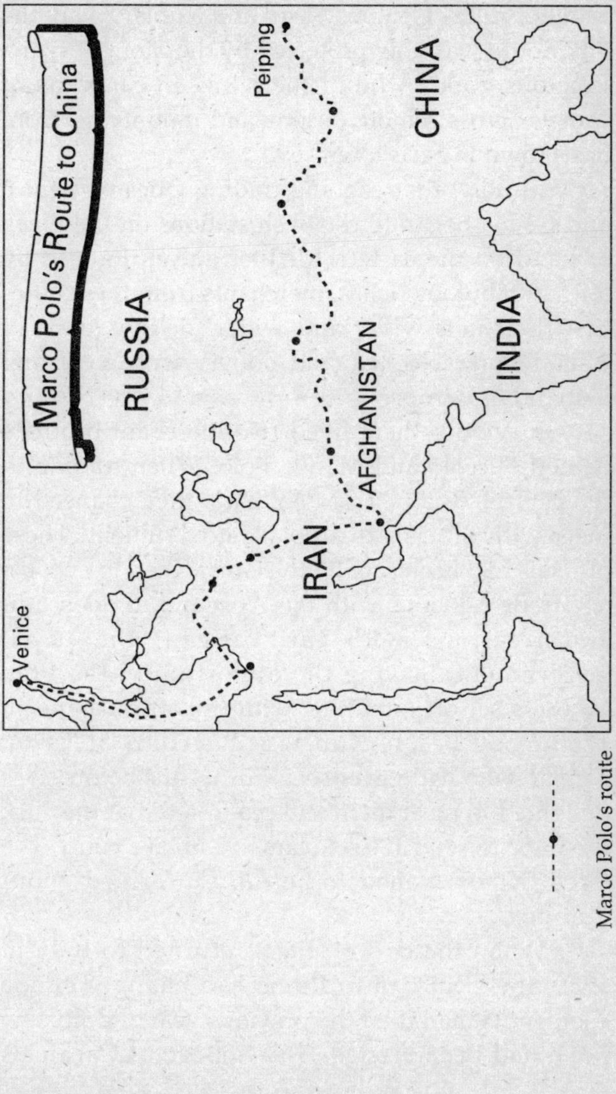
Marco Polo's Route to China
RUSSIA
CHINA
INDIA
AFGHANISTAN
IRAN
Venice
Peiping
Marco Polo's route

Mongol rulers Genghis Khan and Kublai Khan, the Silk Route was now protected by the Mongol army. Precious goods wound their way in caravans of camels across remote deserts and mountains, from oasis town to oasis town.

In Italy, the seagoing trading cities of Venice and Genoa began to establish stations on the Black Sea and on the eastern Mediterranean. Enticed by tales of fabulous riches, merchants from these cities cast their nets wider and wider for the goods of Asia. Silk, spices, tea, and pottery were in strong demand in Europe.

In Venice there lived two merchant brothers named Niccoló and Maffeo Polo. When trading in the central Asian city of Bukhara, they chanced to meet with officials of Kublai's government. These officials had been sent by the Great Khan to encourage trade relations with the West and to open official relations with the Vatican, the papal government. Seizing the opportunity, the Polo brothers set off for China with the officials and in 1260 stood before Kublai at his court at Ta-tu. Kublai, who had never seen Europeans before, was delighted to meet them and requested that they ask the pope to send 100 scholars to Kublai's court. The Great Khan wished to be fully informed about Europe.

When the two brothers returned to Italy in 1269, the situation in Rome had changed. Pope Clement IV had died the previous year and no new pope had been elected. The College of Cardinals could not settle on a successor. After waiting for two years, their frustration mounted. The Polos desired to return to Kublai Khan's court as quickly as possible. (The Polos called China *Cathay*, a word derived from the Turkish *Khitai* or *Kitat*, the name of the people who had ruled over northern China during the 11th century.)

Finally, in 1271, the Polo brothers set off again for the lands of the Great Khan. They had obtained neither the papal blessing nor the 100 scholars Kublai had requested. They did, however, bring something that Kublai was to treasure highly. The Polos brought with them Niccoló's son, Marco. Marco, who was 17 years old, was eager for adventure. He was enthralled by tales of the faraway Asian lands, listened carefully as his father and uncle described their first meeting with Kublai Khan, and yearned to see the Great Khan's court for himself. The three Polos reached Kublai's court in 1275.

All trades of that time had to conduct their business in many languages, and the Polos were no exception. Marco, who was more of a young scholar than a merchant and who was determined to make a good impression on Kublai, at once set about mastering the Mongol tongue. He practised each day, enlarging his vocabulary and polishing his accent. When the Polos reached Kublai's summer residence at Shang-tu and Marco was presented to the Great Khan, he had already prepared a speech of greeting in Kublai's own tongue.

The meeting was a success, especially for the young Marco. A court official later wrote: "They knelt before him and made obeisance with the utmost humility. The Great Khan bade them rise and received them honourably and entertained them with good cheer. He asked many questions about their condition and how they had fared after their departure.... When the Great Khan saw Marco, he asked who he was. 'Sire,' said Messer Niccoló, 'he is my son, and your liege[1] man.' 'He is heartily welcome,' said the Khan."

Marco for his part was favourably impressed by the Khan and described him as "a man of good stature, neither short nor tall but of moderate height. His limbs are well fleshed out and modelled in due proportion. His complexion is fair and ruddy like a rose, the eyes black and handsome, the nose shapely and set squarely in place."

The Polos were housed in the palace at Ta-tu. Marco would call the city Khan-balik, meaning the city of the Great Khan. He immediately set about learning more of the different languages spoken throughout the lands that Kublai ruled. From the eighth century onward, Arabs, Turks, and Persians had settled in large numbers in the northwest and in the ports of southeast China, serving as intermediaries in the commerce by land and by sea across Eurasia.

Marco shared with Kublai a passion for falconry, the training of falcons to hunt, a sport that was popular among the aristocracy of Europe, the

Middle East, and Asia. Kublai invited Marco to accompany him on a hunting expedition. Hunting for the Mongols was a way to train soldiers and reveal a person's character, and the Great Khan carefully observed Marco's conduct during the hunt to test his abilities and learn his temperament. On a typical hunt, as Marco described it, the Khan "stood on top of a wooden tower, full of crossbowmen and archers, which was carried by four elephants wearing stout leather armour draped with cloths of silk and gold. Above his head flew his banner with the emblem of the sun and moon, so high that it could be clearly seen on every side." So impressed was Kublai with this young man that he immediately took Marco into his service.

Marco would serve Kublai as a friend and close adviser for 17 years. The Khan had faith in Marco's honesty and his keen powers of observation and would frequently send him on inspection tours of the empire. Unlike many earlier rulers of China, Kublai was always anxious to hear about the life of his subjects and the conditions under which they lived. For Marco too, it was the perfect opportunity to explore and learn about this vast country.

Marco was fascinated by the things he saw in China that were unknown in Europe. Among the many wonders he described were coal, "a sort of black stone, which is dug out of veins in hillsides and burns like logs," and asbestos, which Marco called "salamander." From China, the Europeans of this time would also learn of gunpowder, and from Chinese noodles the Italians would learn to make pasta.

In his travels Marco began to put together a complete economic and geographic sketch of Kublai's realm, describing the trade and wealth of the Great Khan's empire as well as a number of curiosities at Kublai's court. Later, he would write for European readers that "the revenue accruing to the Great Khan ... is so stupendous that, unless it were seen, it could scarcely be credited." And sure enough, many did not believe, nicknaming the explorer Marco "Millions" for his extravagant tales of the wealth of China.

Kublai recognized the importance of commerce and offered merchants a higher social status than they had enjoyed under the previous Sung dynasty. During the years of the Mongol conquests, merchant associations had raised money for loans to Mongol nobility. Now Kublai rewarded them. To facilitate trade, he revived the Sung use of paper money, forcing all gold and silver to be turned over to the court. "It is in this city of Khan-balik that the Great Khan has his mint," wrote Marco, "and it is so organized that you might well say that he has mastered the art of alchemy [transforming metal into gold]." Marco compared the bustling markets of Chinese cities with those of the great ports of the Western world, such as Venice, his home. Coming from Venice, Marco was particularly impressed with the Chinese system of transporting goods by water and with the Grand Canal that Kublai had built in order to ship grain to his capital at Ta-tu from southern China.

Marco also described the system of paved roads the Khan had built to connect the far reaches of his empire. "Along the main highways frequented by his messengers and by merchants and other folk, he has ordered trees to be planted on both sides, two paces distant from one another. They are so large that they can be seen from a long way off. And he has done this so that any wayfarer may recognize the roads and not lose his way ... they are a great boon to travellers and traders."

Even today, Marco's description of Kublai's New Year's celebrations stretch the imagination. "On this day the Great Khan receives gifts of more than 100 000 white horses of great beauty and price. And on this day also there is a procession of his elephants, fully 5000 in number, all draped in fine cloths embroidered with beasts and birds. Each one bears on its back two strong-boxes of great beauty and price filled with the Khan's plate and with costly apparel for his white-robed court. With them come innumerable camels also draped with cloths and laden with provisions for the feast. They all parade in front of the Great Khan, and it is the most splendid sight that ever was seen. On the morning of this feast, before the tables are set up, all the kings and all the dukes, marquises and counts, barons, knights, astrologers, physicians, falconers, and many other officials and rulers of men and lands and armies appear before the Khan in the great hall.... And when they are all seated, each in his proper station, up stands a great dignitary and proclaims in a loud voice: 'Bow down and worship!' No sooner has he said this than they bow down, then and there, and touch the ground with their foreheads, and address a prayer to the lord and worship him as if he were a god."

Marco served at the court of the Great Khan for 17 years. But the Great Khan was growing old. Kublai had enforced a regime tolerant of all people and religions, but nobody knew how foreigners would be treated by the next ruler. Besides, Marco was now in his 30s. He had worked in Kublai's service for almost half his life. It was time to go home.

When Marco made his wishes known, Kublai was reluctant at first to let his trusted friend leave. Finally, after several more requests, Kublai granted Marco permission to return to Venice after one more mission in his service. Marco was to accompany a newly married Mongol princess to the home of her new husband in Persia. Having discharged this last duty faithfully, Marco and his father Niccoló and his uncle Maffeo, after an extraordinary journey, arrived back in Italy in 1295.

When the Polos returned home, neither friends nor family recognized the three men, who were clothed in shabby garments after their long and arduous journey. Finally, the family was convinced that the three ragged travellers were indeed their returned relatives. They gave orders for a splendid feast to be prepared. At the end of the banquet, the story goes, the three men, still clothed in their tattered garments, ripped open the seams of their coats to let fall a shower of emeralds, diamonds, and rubies that Kublai had presented to them upon their departure from China.

After three years in Venice, Marco volunteered to serve as a "gentleman commander" aboard a Venetian galley in the war against Venice's old trading rival, the city of Genoa. He was captured in a naval battle and sent to a Genoese prison. Here, to pass the time, he told his fellow prisoners about his adventures in the service of Kublai Khan. Among the prisoners was Rusticello of Pisa, a romance writer of considerable fame. Marco dictated his story to Rusticello, and with the Pisan's help, Marco Polo's *Book of Wonders* took form.

1. **liege**: servant

MUHAMMAD IBN-BATUTA TRAVELS THE WORLD

by William Scheller

Who are the great explorers? People who go to places unfamiliar to them? That's one definition. But this 14th-century Arab explorer became famous for travelling to cities and palaces that already existed.

Ibn-Batuta is remembered not for a single trip he took, but for a lifetime of travelling. Indeed, his life was one long exploration of his world. Also, like the great Italian traveller Marco Polo, he had a fine talent for looking sharply at anything he saw and for remembering it so he could tell about it later. Much of what we know about life in the places he visited, in his far-off time, comes from the stories of his travels.

Muhammad ibn-Abdullah ibn-Batuta was born in 1304, in the Moroccan city of Tangier on the Strait of Gibraltar—the narrow body of water that separates North Africa from Spain. Although Morocco was his home, he really belonged to a much larger world. By the 1300s, all of North

Africa, the Middle East, and southern Asia as far as India and Indonesia were united by belief in the Muslim religion, called Islam. Ibn-Batuta spent much of his life exploring this Islamic world.

Ibn-Batuta's earliest travels came about because of his Muslim religion. At least once in his life, every Muslim is supposed to visit Mecca, in Arabia. The pilgrimage to this holiest city of Islam is called the *hajj*. In 1325, after studying to be a lawyer like most of the men in his family, ibn-Batuta decided to make the hajj. For someone living 4827 km from Mecca, this was a big decision, since the journey would take a year or more. For ibn-Batuta, his pilgrimage was the beginning of a trip that would last 24 years!

The 21-year-old lawyer left Tangier in June 1325, and did not reach Mecca until October of the next year. Even in those days, 16 months was a long time for travelling 4827 km. But the places along the way, as well as the place where he was going, interested ibn-Batuta. He stopped for a while in Tunisia, on the north coast of Africa. Then, after crossing the Libyan Desert, he visited the great Egyptian cities of Alexandria and Cairo. At Cairo, and later at the ancient city of Damascus, in Syria, ibn-Batuta visited famous Muslim colleges and studied with learned men.

Leaving Damascus, ibn-Batuta joined a caravan and crossed the fearsome Arabian Desert to reach the holy city of Mecca. (A caravan is a group of people who travel together by camel and on foot. This was how ibn-Batuta moved about through much of his life, and it is still the way some people cross the deserts of Africa and Asia today.)

Once he had made his visit to Mecca's holy places and performed his religious duties, ibn-Batuta made the greatest decision of his life. He would not go straight home to Tangier. Instead, he would keep travelling. Content with his choice, ibn-Batuta joined a caravan that was leaving for Baghdad, which is north of Arabia, in the land now called Iraq.

Ibn-Batuta was the sort of traveller who never went anywhere in a straight line, if there was anything interesting to turn his attention. He had heard about the beautiful cities of Persia (today called Iran) and went east to visit them before turning west to Baghdad. In Baghdad, he became friends with government officials, who invited him to go with them to other cities in Persia. Because of his good education and pleasing manner, ibn-Batuta was often able to meet learned and important people. They made travelling easier for him and helped show him the glories of Muslim civilization in the places where it had been born.

By the time ibn-Batuta had finished touring Persia and Iraq, the season of year for the hajj had come around once again. Being a religious man, he went again to Mecca in 1327. Ibn-Batuta had now been away from home for three years and he needed a rest. So, he decided to stay in Mecca for a year, studying and talking with other travellers, until the time came to continue his journey.

Up until this next adventure, ibn-Batuta had

always travelled by land. Now he would take his first sea voyage, down the Red Sea between Arabia and Egypt. He headed for Yemen, at the southern tip of the Arabian peninsula. Beyond Yemen, a much larger sea stretched to the south. This was the Indian Ocean, which Arab traders sailed on their way to Asia and Africa.

In the time of ibn-Batuta, people did not simply decide when they wanted to travel and then make their plans with ship owners and caravan leaders. Travel was nothing like it is today, when ships, planes, and trains leave at regular, scheduled times. Hundreds of years ago, people and goods moved according to the season, instead of the clock. The great caravans would leave from Cairo and Damascus because the time of year for the hajj had come. Captains would sail their ships out into the Indian Ocean because it was the season when the winds blew in the right direction. And there was no way that ibn-Batuta could call ahead to arrange a place for himself on a ship. A traveller like ibn-Batuta had to go to a seaport and ask until he found a captain willing to take a passenger. He had to be ready to sail when the captain was ready.

That is what ibn-Batuta did in 1329. He travelled to the southern Arabian port of Aden. There he found a trading ship that was headed down the coast of east Africa. Ibn-Batuta was by now collecting places almost as one might collect stamps, and we can imagine how eager he must have been to see one of the most unusual parts of the Muslim world. When the ship reached Mogadishu, in what is now Somalia, and then sailed even farther south across the equator to the country we now call Tanzania, the young man got his first look at towns where most of the Muslims were black Africans. Islam, he must have been proud to see, had indeed spread far.

From Africa, ibn-Batuta sailed north again to Arabia and by a zigzag route got himself back to Mecca in the year 1330. Mecca, by now, was for him more than a holy place. It was his favourite spot for resting and collecting his thoughts between trips.

And the trips grew longer and longer. His new plan was to sail to India, but he had trouble finding someone in Arabia who knew India and could go with him as a guide. So he decided to travel by land. Perhaps he would meet a guide along the way.

The land route ibn-Batuta chose began in Turkey, which he reached by sailing in a merchant ship on the Mediterranean Sea. Here was yet another land and yet another kind of people, and once again the traveller's attention was turned. He wandered all over the Turkish peninsula, even taking side trips across the Black Sea to what is now the country of Ukraine (in the former Soviet Union) and to the great Christian city of Constantinople. This surely wasn't the quick way to India! But because ibn-Batuta took so much extra time, he was able to learn about a part of the world that was changing very quickly. The Turks were growing more powerful, and the empire of

Constantinople—the Byzantine Empire—was growing weaker. In another 120 years, the Turks would conquer Constantinople, and it would be a Christian city no longer. Today, it is the Turkish city of Istanbul.

When ibn-Batuta finally pointed himself in the direction of India, he travelled along one of history's most famous trade routes. Since ancient times, the caravan roads across central Asia had been busy with traders carrying Chinese silks and spices from the Indies. Now, with his horses and camels, servants and friends, ibn-Batuta crossed the broad Asian plains and made his way through the mountain passes of Afghanistan. By September 1333, he was in India.

When he set out for India, ibn-Batuta already had a plan in mind. He had heard that the Muslim ruler, or *sultan,* of northern India liked to give important jobs to learned Muslims from other lands, and ibn-Batuta felt he might be just the sort of person the sultan was looking for. Ibn-Batuta had been away from home for eight years. He was not a poor man to begin with, and during his travels, he had been helped with presents and gifts of money from rich people who felt it was their duty to help a travelling scholar. But by now, he probably wanted to earn money on his own. He had studied law and could work as a lawyer or judge anywhere where Muslim law was the rule.

Ibn-Batuta found what he wanted. The sultan, Mohammed Tughluk, asked him to become a judge. But he had to promise to stay at the capital city of Delhi. He did stay—for eight years. Toward the end of that time, however, he grew afraid of the sultan, a dangerous man who sometimes turned against his friends and officials. When the sultan asked ibn-Batuta to go to China and give his greetings to the Chinese emperor, the traveller was glad to do so.

This was the unluckiest trip of ibn-Batuta's life. On the way to the coast, where his party was to set sail for China, he was attacked by Hindu rebels. Ibn-Batuta was captured, but escaped after almost being killed. Then, after nearly everyone in the party, except ibn-Batuta and a few others, had boarded the ships, a storm wrecked the fleet and all the ships were lost—along with all the precious gifts ibn-Batuta was supposed to give to the Chinese emperor. Ibn-Batuta was sure of one thing: he did not want to go back to Delhi with this news.

Instead, he set sail for the Maldive Islands, which lie in the Arabian Sea 644 km southwest of India. There, he made friends with the local ruler and again became a judge. This time, however, he stayed in one place for less than a year.

Between 1344 and 1347, ibn-Batuta travelled east of India, to what is now the country of Bangladesh and to the island of Sumatra in Indonesia. Finally, he reached China. We don't know how far he really got into China, but one thing is sure—he travelled far enough to realize that he had passed the limits of the world he knew. China was as strange a land as any he had seen. He wrote later about odd Chinese things like paper money and about how surprised he was that the roads were safe from robbers. But he did not feel at ease in this beautiful land. Here, the only other Muslims he met were traders in the port cities. He had finally gone beyond the Muslim world.

The time had come to return home. Between the years 1347 and 1349, ibn-Batuta made his way west, passing through India, Persia, Syria, and Arabia, where he made the hajj to Mecca once again. From there, he travelled to Egypt, where he began the last part of his trip by ship along the coast of North Africa. Near the end of 1349, he arrived home in Tangier. He had been 21 when he left. Now he was 45. His mother and father, he learned, were dead.

Ibn-Batuta took only two more trips. One was to southern Spain, where Muslim rulers were still in power. The other was longer and more dangerous, taking him south across the Sahara Desert to the African kingdom of Mali. When he returned from that final trip, in 1354, the sultan of Morocco asked him to write the story of his travels. This he did, with the help of a younger man. And then ibn-Batuta settled into a quiet life as a lawyer or a judge. In the 15 years he had left to live, he may have wondered how many people knew about his stories and believed them. How surprised ibn-Batuta would be to learn that those stories are still being read more than 600 years later!

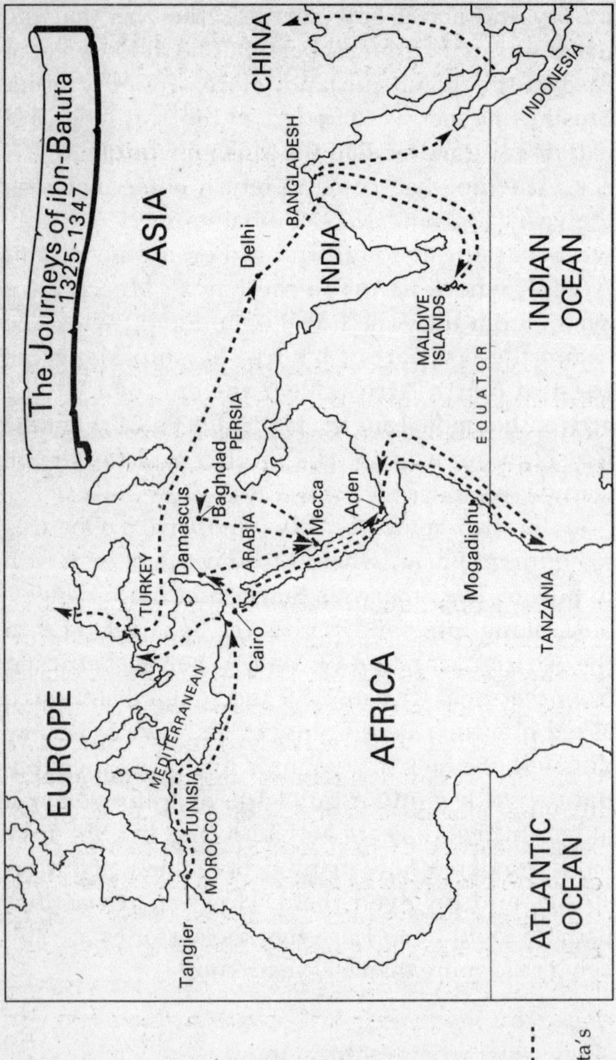

ibn-Batuta's route

THE BLACK DEATH CHANGES EUROPE

from Reader's Digest *Quest for the Past*

In our own time, most diseases have been kept under control by modern medicine, preventing them from becoming epidemics. But throughout history infectious diseases have swept the world, killing millions of people.

The worst human disaster in history was not a 20th-century world war. It was the 14th-century plague known as the Black Death. In Europe alone a full quarter of the population—some 25 million people—died within the space of four years (1347–51). Today it is thought that this devastation (like that of similar later epidemics) was started by bacteria carried by fleas lodged in the hair of a type of far-ranging rat that flourishes in almost any habitat. Human beings catch the disease either from the bite of the fleas or from the bodily discharges of infected persons. To people of the 14th century, however, the plague looked like nothing less than God's terrible punishment for humanity's sins.

From Central Asia the horror travelled to the Crimea with trade caravans, thence by ship to Mediterranean coasts, and onward, remorselessly, across Europe. Normal life ceased. Fields were left untilled, cattle turned loose to fend for themselves. Corpses were soon being buried, one on top of another, in shallow graves, tipped into pits, or even left rotting in the streets. City life ground to a halt as contagion spread and people fled from their homes. The air seemed polluted with what one contemporary chronicle describes as "an unbearable stench ... so fetid as to be overpowering."

Only a few places were spared. In Milan, for instance, the archbishop ordered that, if the infection reached the city, the first three houses where it appeared must immediately be walled up, with the dead, sick, and healthy all entombed within. This was done—and Milan suffered no further. The archbishop, without knowing how the pestilence had spread, had nevertheless hit upon a reliable barrier to it: Isolation. Thus an isolated country house might be a good sanctuary. The writer Giovanni Boccaccio sets his *Decameron* (c. 1353) in a palace where 10 aristocratic young people gather to avoid plague-stricken Florence. There, while waiting for the danger to recede, they amuse themselves by telling stories. Segregation could also work on a larger scale. Vast tracts of present-day Poland were spared, perhaps partly because Polish authorities imposed a quarantine.

It was isolation, too, that saved Pope Clement

VI, then resident in Avignon, France. On the advice of his doctors he withdrew to a private apartment, where, despite the warmth of summer, he sat in solitude for weeks between two enormous fires kept permanently stoked. Although the doctors could not have known it, their advice made medical sense, for the great heat repelled fleas. Fire also preserved a certain English nobleman who ruthlessly ordered a nearby village to be burned down when it was attacked by the plague. Neither the flames nor the fleas reached his own property.

Apart from such rare instances, the plague took a dreadful toll as it swept through Europe. Yet we see that, during the course of history, such appalling loss of life has often been preceded by economic hardship owing to the pressure of overpopulation. Catastrophes on a large scale, such as the plague and international wars, have tended to follow on from the problem of overcrowding. Through the centuries, this problem has been solved—not by governments' economic policies—but by "accidental" and enormous loss of life. After the Black Death, the relationship between master and servant changed significantly. With a quarter of Europe's population destroyed, workers could ask for higher wages, while landowners, faced with less demand for basic commodities such as grain, had to accept lower prices. The resultant economic and social ferment led to sporadic disturbances, particularly among the lower classes, occasionally culminating in uprisings.

Unfortunately, the improvement in the peasant's lot that resulted from the plague was relatively short-lived. By the 16th century, the rapid rise in population meant that the peasantry were even worse off in terms of real wages.

How They Fought The Plague

Physicians in the 14th century were not wholly unskilled. They could remove teeth, set bones, even do skin grafts. In the face of the plague, though, they were powerless. And unaware of its cause, they could only guess at treatments.

The disease takes one of three forms. It may be bubonic, chiefly characterized by swelling of lymph nodes (buboes, or boils) in the armpits, groin, and site of the flea bite. It may be pneumonic, infecting the lungs and causing the coughing up of blood. Or—most deadly of all types—it may be septicemic, a form in which the bloodstream is rapidly invaded by offending bacteria and death is inevitable within hours.

Confronted with widely differing symptoms, contemporary doctors usually began by trying to draw "poison" from the body by means of bleeding, laxatives, and enemas. Buboes were either lanced or covered with hot plasters. Various haphazard potions ranging from powdered stag's horn to rare spices and compounds of gold were prescribed. Aromatic woods were burned to purify the air, and floors were sprinkled with rosewater and vinegar—measures that succeeded only in masking the stench of decaying flesh.

To forestall attacks, a variety of diets were recommended, and some may actually have been beneficial by making people fitter and therefore more able to fight infection. But the best safeguard was thought to be a mind at peace with God. In fact, the physician took second place to the priest in the sickroom, for the afflicted were always prayed over and given confession before they could have medical treatment. Sick people tended to welcome this, for they knew their plight was hopeless and, despairing, wished for a place in a future world when this world's medicines failed. Not everyone died of the plague. But when stricken people recovered, their survival was normally hailed as a miracle.

Many further outbreaks of the plague have occurred since the Black Death, but only in our own century have we discovered the source of the scourge and its antidote. When the virulent epidemic of 1665 reached London, physicians were not much better equipped to fight it than their earlier counterparts had been. The 17th-century plague, details of which are graphically depicted in the famous *Diary* of Samuel Pepys, took scores of thousands of lives in London alone. Ironically, one 17th-century solution for the problem involved the wholesale murder of dogs and cats—the very creatures that might have helped to slim down the rat population.

FIVE TERRIBLE EPIDEMICS

by Deborah G. Felder

Plague Of Justinian

Byzantine Empire, 500–650 C.E.

The bubonic plague, a deadly disease spread by rodents and transmitted to humans by fleas, raged through the Byzantine Empire during the reign of Justinian I. An estimated 100 million people died of the plague.

Smallpox

Mexico and Central America, 1500 and after

This highly contagious disease was brought to the New World by the Spanish conquistadors. It caused the deaths of several million Indians in Mexico and Central America—possibly as much as half the population. Smallpox has been around since the beginning of human history. The last major epidemic occurred in India and Pakistan in 1967. The United Nation's World Health Organization mounted a huge campaign in the 1960s to rid the world of smallpox, and by the late 1970s, the disease had been largely eradicated.

Europeans also introduced another disease to Mexican Indians in the 1500s—measles. In the epidemic of 1530–1545, some 1 million to 1.5 million Indians died from measles, to which they had no immunity.

Saint Anthony's Fire

Russia, 1722

Also called Holy Fire, the scientific name of this disease is ergotism. It is an infection of the nervous system caused by a fungus, ergota, that grows on rye and other cereal grains. In 1722, 20 000 Russians died from eating bread made from diseased rye. Many of the victims were soldiers camped along the Volga River preparing for Tsar Peter the Great's invasion of the western lands. So many troops died that Peter had to call off the invasion.

Polio

North America, 1916 and 1946

Poliomyelitis, or Infantile Paralysis, is a viral disease that often causes paralysis of arms, legs, and muscles that control swallowing, heartbeat, and breathing. There were outbreaks of the disease all through the first half of the 20th century, but the worst epidemics took place in 1916 (27 363 cases) and 1946 (25 191 cases). Many people died from the disease, but most became disabled. Those who could not breathe were placed in iron lungs, a device that rhythmically expands and contracts the chest muscles causing artificial breathing. An Australian nurse, Sister Elizabeth Kenny, came up with a successful physical therapy treatment for polio. Hot, moist applications were used, together with mild exercise, to stimulate paralyzed arms and legs. But the real breakthrough came in 1955, when the first polio vaccine was created by Dr. Jonas Salk. The Salk vaccine and the Sabin oral vaccine (created by Dr. Albert Sabin) of 1960 practically eradicated polio in the United States.

Spanish Influenza

Worldwide, 1918–1919

No one is sure where this deadly form of the flu (short for "influenza") originally came from, but it was first identified as a virus at Fort Riley, Kansas. The epidemic began there in March, 1918, during World War I, and quickly spread to other army camps across the United States. In April the flu hit American soldiers at Brest, France, and then spread throughout Europe and the rest of the world. The flu struck Spain so hard that the disease was named "Spanish Influenza." The only areas of the world to escape the epidemic were the Atlantic islands of Tristan de Cunha and St. Helena and the Pacific island of New Guinea. By the time the Spanish Flu mysteriously vanished in 1919, over 20 million people had died.

JOAN OF ARC FIGHTS FOR FRANCE

from *Great Lives*

As a young girl, Joan became convinced that it was her mission to save France from the English and to have Charles, the Dauphin (or eldest son of the French king), crowned as king. From then on it seemed that nothing and nobody could stop her.

The Hundred Years' War between England and France began when the English King Edward III claimed the French throne for himself in 1337. For the next 113 years, through the reigns of five French and five English kings, the two countries fought over the issue. Joan of Arc entered the war at a turning point. At a moment when the French lacked strong leadership and seemed threatened on all sides, she inspired a great victory at the siege of Orléans and turned the tide of the war in favour of France.

Joan was born in the tiny village of Domrémy in the region of northern France called Champagne.

Although she had no schooling of any kind, she was an intelligent child. When she was nine years old the English army occupied the area around her home, remaining for almost three years. When she was 13 she began hearing "voices" telling her to go to France's rescue. Convinced that she had received a command from God, Joan managed to get an audience with the Dauphin Charles, the heir to the French throne as the former king's eldest son. He was at first suspicious of her, and so disguised himself and hid among a crowd of his attendants listening to her speak. Joan, although she had never seen him before, is said to have recognized him immediately. This convinced Charles that she really had received a command from heaven. She was given a magnificent suit of armour and was sent to join the army.

On April 29, 1429, she arrived at the city of Orléans, which was besieged by the English army. Within 10 days Joan had chased the English out of the city and forced them to retreat. Inspired by her leadership and determination, Charles and the French army marched through English territory to the city of Rheims, where Charles was crowned king in July.

Joan now tried to persuade Charles to press home his advantage and defeat the English once and for all, but she found that the new king was satisfied with what had been achieved and unwilling to fight any more. So Joan herself led an army to the south. It was then that she was captured and sold to the English. After nine months in prison, she was brought to trial by a religious court for heresy and sorcery. The charges were absurd, but Joan was found guilty and sentenced to death. On May 30, 1431, she was burned at the stake in the marketplace of the city of Rouen. Charles had done nothing to help her, although later he tried to persuade the Pope to overturn the guilty verdict. This was finally done in 1456; in 1920 she was declared a saint.

Joan of Arc's Life

1412	Joan is born January 6 at Domrémy.
1421	English army occupies area around Joan's home (they leave in 1424).
1425	Joan receives message from heaven to rescue France from the English.
1429	March: Joan persuades Charles to allow her to join the French army.
	April 29: Joan leads French army in defeating the English at the siege of Orléans.
	July 17: Charles crowned Charles VII of France at Rouen.
1431	Joan attempts to relieve region of Compiègne. She is captured and sold to the English.
	February 21: Joan's trial for witchcraft and heresy begins.
	May 30: Joan burned at the stake in Rouen.

MOCTEZUMA RULES THE AZTECS

by Frances F. Berdan

When the Native people of Mexico arrived in the Valley of Mexico and built the city of Tenochtitlan (where Mexico City now stands), a glorious civilization was unfolding. Years later, in 1519, as the ruler, Moctezuma, (called Montezuma by the Spaniards) greeted Cortés of Spain, he could not have expected the devastation that would follow.

It is November 1519. Just outside Tenochtitlan, one of the world's great cities, two powerful men approach each other. As they meet, one offers a greeting by touching his hand to the ground and kissing it; the other offers an embrace but is rebuffed. The first, wearing a beautifully decorated cotton cape and sheltered by a canopy made of gleaming gold ornaments and shimmering green feathers, is the Aztec ruler Moctezuma. The other, more simply dressed in metal armour, is the Spanish captain Hernando Cortés.

It is a tense encounter. This solemn meeting marks the beginning of a dramatic clash between the Aztecs and the Spaniards.

The people we call Aztecs actually called themselves Mexica. Mexico, therefore, is the land of the Mexica. They built Tenochtitlan, their greatest city, on an island in the Valley of Mexico; it is now completely covered by Mexico City. The Mexica travelled to the Valley of Mexico from northern lands. When they arrived there, they found it already densely populated. Their search for a home ended in 1325 on a small island in a huge lake, where they saw an eagle with a snake in its mouth perched on a cactus. These elements make up the central symbol of the Mexican flag.

The city grew rapidly, and by the year 1519, it contained between 150 000 and 200 000 people. The island itself was quite small, however, and had room only for temples, palaces, and government buildings. Thus, the people constructed *chinampas*, or "floating gardens," to give them space to plant their crops. These gardens did not really float but were made of many layers of mud and vegetation. Canals and footpaths separated the plots of land. Farmers then built their houses on the land and harvested food and flowers for residents of the city.

In addition to farming, some city dwellers fished in the lake and made goods such as pottery, baskets, and cloth. Others, such as doctors, load carriers, and matchmakers, provided needed services, while still others prepared food for sale in the marketplace. Most girls learned at an early age to cook, spin thread, weave cloth, and tend children. These activities, along with buying and selling goods in the busy marketplace, occupied a woman's life before and after marriage and into old age.

Beside these producers and labourers, the population included wealthy and high-ranking merchants and artisans who made fancy and expensive goods. The merchants travelled long distances into often dangerous lands, especially to tropical lands to the east and south of the Valley of Mexico. They usually travelled in caravans, on foot or in canoes, in search of bright tropical feathers, colourfully decorated clothing, precious stones such as jadeite, ornaments made of gold and silver, and cacao (chocolate) beans. Cacao was the most prized drink of the land, but the beans also were used as a form of money, like small change.

The merchants brought back many materials that the artisans used to make luxury items. The stoneworkers made complicated mosaic masks, necklaces, and other personal adornments; the metalworkers fashioned gold and silver into art objects and jewellery; and the feather workers spent long hours making fans, shields, and headdresses. These fancy adornments were to be worn only by nobles, people in the highest ranks of the society.

To be a noble, one had to be born of noble parents. Noblemen had many rights not given to other people, including the right to attend a special school, the right to have many wives, and the right to engage in the most powerful occupations. Most powerful were the ruler and his advisors. Other nobles could become teachers, government administrators, captains and generals in the military, and priests. Noblewomen often managed large households in grand palaces.

There were two types of schools. Those for commoners (not nobles) taught boys the art of war. Those for nobles taught military skills and also provided instruction in history, astronomy, astrology, writing, and philosophy. They trained boys to work in the government, priesthood, and military. Since the Mexica controlled a huge empire covering most of central and southern Mexico by 1519, many officials—such as tribute collectors, governors, and ambassadors—were required. And since the Mexica and their neighbours worshiped many gods who controlled, among other things, rain, warfare, and corn, they needed many priests.

The Mexica were almost always waging war, and the nobles occupied the highest military ranks. They conquered many other peoples in Mexico, bringing home enemy warriors for sacrifice to their gods, as well as booty and tributes for their palaces and homes. Farmers and other commoners often were taken from their everyday activities to serve as warriors on some faraway battlefield. Warriors who showed extraordinary courage and skill received special rewards from the ruler, and a few were invited to join knightly orders such as the eagle or jaguar warriors.

Less than two years after Moctezuma and Cortés met in 1519, the Spaniards conquered the proud Aztec warriors and, as new lords of the land, changed forever the Aztecs' way of life.

The great Aztec city of Tenochtitlan was conquered by the Spaniards after a siege that lasted 80 days. The capital city was burnt to the ground and soon the rest of the empire fell under Spanish control. The Aztecs were experienced warriors who fought fiercely to defend their way of life, but they had no way of fighting against new diseases brought by the Europeans. An epidemic of smallpox swept across Mexico. Fifty years after the Spaniards arrived, war and disease had reduced the Native population of Central America to one-tenth of what it was at the time of Moctezuma's meeting with Cortés.

TAJ MAHAL, A LOVE POEM IN MARBLE

by Leah Eskin

It's been called the world's most beautiful building and humanity's closest brush with perfection. But more than anything else, India's Taj Mahal stands as a testament to one man's enduring love.

Glistening like a perfect gem set into the heart of Agra, India, the Taj Mahal inspires the most lavish of praise. It has been called one of the modern seven wonders of the world, the world's most beautiful building, and humanity's closest brush with perfection.

But the glory of the white marble monument lies not only in its elegant design and extraordinary craftsmanship. For 400 years, the Taj Mahal has stood as a testament to a story of enduring love.

The story begins in 1526 when Babar, a Muslim ruler from what is now Afghanistan, invaded and conquered the ancient Hindu land of India. During the next 200 years, Babar's descendants, known as the Mogul emperors, stretched their power across most of the land that is now Bangladesh, India, Pakistan, Afghanistan, and Nepal.

The Mogul Empire brought India peace, stability, and a renowned cultural life. Babar's grandson, Akbar, the greatest of the emperors, won respect for his keen sense of justice and his belief in religious tolerance for the empire's Hindu majority.

At the height of the Mogul reign, in 1628, Akbar's grandson Shah Jahan took the throne. The young emperor served as a patron of the arts, encouraging both Hindu and Islamic architecture to flourish. Hindus decorated their temples with carved sculptures of their gods. Muslims, forbidden by their religion to carve the human figure, decorated their mosques with quotations from the Koran, Islam's holy book.

Like his predecessors, Shah Jahan had many wives. But his most cherished was Arjumand Banu, better known by her title of Mumtaz Mahal, or Taj Mahal—the Crown of the Palace. The two were married when Shah Jahan was just 20, and during their 18 years together, they were inseparable. The empress became the ruler's chief political adviser, counsellor, and constant companion. She even followed him into battle to wipe the sweat from his brow. Mumtaz Mahal pleased her husband even more by bearing 14 children. In 1631, while delivering their last child, she died. On her deathbed, she asked her husband to build "a monument of perfect proportions" to symbolize their perfect love.

The grief-stricken emperor complied. He spent the next 20 years creating for his wife a magnificent tomb, the Taj Mahal.

Shah Jahan commissioned an architect from Persia to design the building. He imported turquoise from Tibet, jasper from the Punjab (a region in present-day India and Pakistan), jade from China, and carnelian (a type of quartz) from Arabia. He shipped hundreds of tonnes of pure white marble to Agra, his capital city. He hired 20 000 jewellers, builders, masons, and calligraphers. The craftsmen toiled for two decades to assemble a masterpiece of perfect proportions.

The completed monument, then as now, rests on a vast platform, 609 m long and 305 m wide. At each of the four corners stands a three-storey minaret, or Muslim prayer tower.

In the centre, the domed mausoleum, a glistening white shrine encrusted with semi-precious jewels, looms above a calm reflecting pool. At its very heart, enclosed by a lacy marble screen, lie the cenotaphs, or burial monuments, to Shah Jahan and Mumtaz Mahal. Directly below, sealed in a vault, rest the remains of the famous lovers.

Actually, Shah Jahan never intended to rest eternally beside his wife. He planned a black marble replica of the Taj Mahal for himself. He dreamed of building it directly across the Jumna River from its white twin. The two were to be joined by a black-and-white bridge across the waters. But in 1658, Shah Jahan fell ill. His son, Aurangzeb, anxious to beat out his brothers to the throne, seized control of the empire. He imprisoned his father in an Agra fortress.

Shah Jahan lived out the rest of his days in the fortress tower, gazing hour after hour at his life's work, the Taj Mahal. His last wish was to be carried to a window, where, one legend says, "dimly looking across the waters at the glowing whiteness and the glittering of that melody in marble, he fell into a deep and endless sleep."

BRITAIN AND FRANCE BATTLE FOR CANADA

by Karen Ford, Janet MacLean, and Barry Wansbrough

Over 200 years ago, Britain and France both had settlers and economic interests in Canada. Their struggle for control led to the deciding battle on the Plains of Abraham—and the deaths of both leaders, General Montcalm and General Wolfe.

In 1756, Britain and France began their Seven Years' War. This was to be their final struggle for control of North America.

In the first years of the war, the French forces held their own. Under their leader, General Montcalm, they captured British forts and defended their lands south of the Great Lakes.

In 1758, the tide began to turn. The British captured Fort Louisbourg, New France's stone fortress on the Atlantic. Then they attacked and captured other French forts, and took control of the Great Lakes.

In 1759, General Wolfe led a British attack on

Quebec. In the dark of night, Wolfe's forces scaled the cliffs upriver from the town. The next morning, the French and British assembled their armies on the Plains of Abraham. After a short fierce battle, Quebec fell.

The next spring, British ships sailed up the St. Lawrence to seal the victory. In the fall, the French surrendered Montreal, their last stronghold on the St. Lawrence. The final battle was fought in 1762, at St. John's, Newfoundland.

The Seven Years' War ended in 1763, with the signing of the Treaty of Paris. Under its terms, Britain took control of most of North America. France kept only the islands of St. Pierre and Miquelon to offer "shelter for French fishermen."

For 150 years, New France had been the setting for drama, glory, and adventure. Its people had suffered incredible hardships to make the wilderness their home. Now, after struggling through so many trials, New France ceased to exist.

The Homesick General

Louis-Joseph de Montcalm was not a soldier at heart. He loved the rolling hills and terraced vineyards of his home in southern France. He much preferred his tranquil fields to the musket-smoke and cannon-fire of war. Montcalm became a soldier to uphold his family's long military tradition. He became an ensign at nine, and fought his first battle at 20. Over the next years, he fought in many wars and was wounded five times.

In 1749, Montcalm retired to his country estate. He spent seven happy years with his wife and young children. Then, in 1756, he was asked to command the French forces in North America. He wanted to refuse, but he agreed for the sake of his duty.

Montcalm sailed to New France and took quick action against the British. He led a force south of the Great Lakes to attack the British forts there. He captured Fort Oswego and took over 16 000 British prisoners. The next year, he captured Fort William Henry, in present-day New York State.

Despite his success, Montcalm was unhappy in the rough colony. "I am deeply desirous of peace," he wrote his wife. "I think I should have given up all my honours to be back with you."

As time passed, Montcalm saw the tide of war turn against him. The British sent more troops and captured Fort Louisbourg on the Atlantic. Montcalm sent to Paris for more soldiers, but the French army was tied up in Europe.

In 1759, General Wolfe led the British up the St. Lawrence. He lay siege to Quebec, but Montcalm defended the city well. Then, in the middle of the night, Wolfe's men scaled the cliffs upriver of Quebec. By morning, they reached the Plains of Abraham, just outside the town. If Montcalm had stayed behind Quebec's walls, he might have saved the day. Other French troops would have arrived to take Wolfe from behind. However, instead of waiting, Montcalm chose to attack.

Montcalm gathered his forces, most of them untrained settlers. Then he mounted his black charger and raised his sword up high. Slowly, he led his men forward into battle.

The British held their ground and fired one volley at the French. Montcalm watched as his lines collapsed in chaos. He swung his horse around and tried to rally his fleeing men.

Suddenly, British grapeshot caught him in the abdomen and thigh. Montcalm managed to stay on his horse with help from his men. He painfully rode to the walls of the city and entered the Saint-Louis Gate.

When the townspeople saw their leader, they came running to his side. People started to cry when they saw his wounds. "It is nothing, nothing at all," said Montcalm gallantly. "Do not grieve on my account, dear friends."

Montcalm died the next morning as dawn broke over the fallen town. He was buried in the Ursuline Convent, in a hole blasted by a British shell. His body rests there still, far from the fields and valleys of his beloved home.

The Conquering General

Up the River St. Lawrence our troops will advance!
To the Grenadiers' March we will teach them to
  dance!
Cape Breton we've taken, the next we will try
At their capital to give them another black eye!

And ye that love fighting will soon have enough!
Wolfe commands us, my boys, we shall give them
hot stuff!

—from "Hot Stuff,"
sung by Wolfe's soldiers

James Wolfe was a pale and sickly boy, but he had the heart of a lion. When he was 13, he volunteered to fight the Spanish with his father's regiment. By the time he was 18, he had fought many battles in distant lands.

In 1758, Wolfe fought in the British siege of Fort Louisbourg. He led a landing party through a storm of musket-fire to gain a British foothold on the shore. Then he led the left wing of the attack to a brilliant victory.

In June 1759, Wolfe sailed up the St. Lawrence to Quebec. He began firing his cannons at the town, but he knew this attack was useless. Quebec was surrounded by stone walls and perched atop high cliffs. As long as the French stayed inside, they would not be beaten.

As the summer passed, Wolfe looked for ways to draw the French into the open. He decided to attack upriver to cut off the French from supplies. He found a dry stream-bed that wound up the cliff-face three kilometres above Quebec.

The night of September 12 was cloudy and dark. Wolfe ordered some of his men to launch a noisy attack as a diversion. Then he and his ships slipped silently away. At four in the morning, the first two dozen men climbed in pairs up the narrow path. At the top, they overpowered some French guards who were sleeping in their tents. Then 4000 Redcoats scaled the cliff, climbing two by two.

By morning, Wolfe's army was standing in battle-line formation on the Plains of Abraham. General Montcalm could scarcely believe his eyes. Rashly, he brought his own army forward to meet the attack.

As the French advanced, Wolfe ordered his front lines to kneel and hold their fire. The French came closer, firing wildly, but still Wolfe held his ground. Then, when the French were within 35 m, he gave the order to fire. Thousands of muskets roared at once, and dense white smoke filled the air. When it cleared, the French lines were in chaos. Hundreds of French lay dead or dying, and others were fleeing back to the town.

Wolfe led his men forward to rout the retreating army. In his brilliant red uniform, he made an easy target. He was shot in the wrist, but he scarcely seemed to notice. He bandaged the wound with his handkerchief and kept on. Another bullet caught Wolfe in the stomach, then another full in the chest. He fell to the ground, mortally wounded. Two of his officers picked him up and carried him gently out of the line of fire.

As Wolfe lay dying, he gave his officers final orders for victory. His last words were those of a true soldier. "Now God be praised," he gasped. "Since I have conquered, I will die in peace."

AUSTRALIA: A PRISON COLONY BECOMES A NATION

by Bob Black

Australia's first people, the Aborigines, lived undisturbed until Captain Cook's voyages of exploration. Then Britain made a decision: it would send British criminals to far-off Australia instead of keeping them in prison. From this strange beginning, a modern nation emerged.

Back in 1643, a Dutch captain named Abel Tasman thought he had sailed around Australia. But he had not stayed in sight of land and had missed much of the coastline. Now the 18th-century voyager Captain James Cook headed south to find the unknown continent and to claim it for Britain.

Captain Cook proved that Tasman had seen New Zealand, not Australia, by charting the coast of the former. He then sailed on to Australia, skirting the coast and charting shores previously unseen by any European. Cook crossed the Great

Barrier Reef and discovered eastern Australia, which he named New South Wales.

Cook also met the inhabitants of the Great Continent. The Europeans called them Aborigines, which means "The First Men." They were a people whose way of life seemed to outsiders not to have changed in thousands of years. This way of life, like that of the peoples of the New World when the first Europeans arrived there, was completely untouched by European civilization.

When Cook finished his survey, he sailed for home, reaching England in 1771. He returned to a country plagued by many problems. At the end of the 18th century, the crime rate in England was soaring. There was no national police force. Such law enforcement as did exist was local and unable to stop crime, though it could catch some of the criminals. Imprisoning criminals meant that society was responsible for feeding and guarding them, and the prisons themselves had to be built and maintained. It was easier and cheaper to send criminals to work in and populate England's colonies.

Previously, about a thousand criminals a year had been shipped to America, but the loss of the American Colonies after the American Revolution meant that criminals could no longer be dumped in the New World. For a time, they were kept offshore on prison ships—rotting hulks that were no longer seaworthy. But this practice was neither satisfactory nor safe. So the British government decided to send convicted thieves, murderers, blackmailers, gamblers, pickpockets, and other criminals to Australia.

Sir Joseph Banks, an accomplished naturalist, had accompanied Cook on his first voyage to the Pacific. He told the British government that Australia's Botany Bay would be perfect for this plan. There were no wild animals, the climate was mild, and the soil was rich. In addition, the native inhabitants were not a threat to colonists. And there was an added benefit: Australia was as far from Britain as possible.

In 1787, eight dilapidated sailing ships assembled in Portsmouth. On board were 717 men and women condemned to make the 48 000-km journey to Australia. Captain Arthur Phillip, commander of the expedition, requested more supplies and equipment for the journey, but the authorities ignored him.

As the expedition left Portsmouth on Sunday, May 13, 1787, a lone clergyman knelt on the shore and prayed for the unfortunates on board. They needed his prayers. Below decks, people were caged like animals. Everyone—men, women, and children—suffered throughout the eight-month journey. When they arrived in Australia, the suffering continued. Botany Bay was no paradise; it was barren rock and sterile sand. The first year, the crops failed and supplies ran out. In 1790, another 759 convicts arrived to swell the colony. Half of them were sick, and the ships brought no new supplies.

America had been settled by free men and women seeking a better life in the New World. In contrast, Australia was forcibly settled by convicts. In 1792, just five settlers arrived of their own free will, and in 1794 the number dropped to two.

The convicts had to learn the skills necessary to keep the colony going. They built villages that were to become towns, as well as businesses and farms. But for the first 40 years, the colony was seen as the "trash can" of the British Empire.

Not until the 1820s did the British government decide to change Australia's image from a dumping ground for criminals to a colony that offered opportunities for free men and women. In 1823, convicts represented 42 percent of the population. By 1841, that number had decreased to 20 percent. The rest of the people were free men and women. That was quite an achievement, for during that 20-year period, 80 percent of all criminals transported to Australia arrived. The government had succeeded in changing Australia's image and had convinced people to emigrate of their own free will.

These new colonists demanded a representative government, and they got it. They also demanded an end to transporting convicts to Australia. In 1840, the governments stopped sending criminals to New South Wales, and the last convicts were shipped to Western Australia in 1867. In all, 170 000 men, women, and children had been forcibly transported to Australia.

Unfortunately, the free people of the new continent did not open their new government and extend its freedoms to the native inhabitants. The Aborigines were treated badly, cheated, and murdered. In Tasmania, they were hunted like wild animals, with dogs and beaters driving them out of the bush, until there were no Aborigines left alive on the island. They survived in other parts of Australia, but always as second-class citizens.

Australia's prosperity came from sheep ranching. By 1850, there were 16 million sheep in Australia—and only 1 million people. In the 1850s, gold was discovered there. The British government claimed that the land was theirs and demanded that miners pay a licence fee. The miners complained and began arming themselves. When they built a stockade, British soldiers put down the rebellion. But the government had learned its lesson from its earlier dealings with America. Licences were abolished and compromises reached.

Today Australia is a modern democracy. But it still maintains close ties with the British, some of whose ancestors were forced to travel 48 000 km to build a new civilization down under.

Time Capsule
THE WINDS OF REVOLUTION

from *Chronicle of the World*

A little more than 200 years ago, almost every country in the world was ruled by a hereditary monarch—a king or queen—and money and power was held in the hands of aristocrats. Then new ideas began to sweep around the world, ideas about equality, liberty, and democracy. How to achieve them? Usually, by violent revolution. Here are some critical moments from the American, French, and Russian Revolutions.

American Independence is Declared

Philadelphia, 4 July 1776

In the words of John Adams, a delegate from Massachusetts, this was the "most memorable epoch in the history of America." He spoke as fellow delegates from 12 of the 13 colonies approved a moving document which declares these colonies independent from Great Britain. Only New York has abstained, but is expected to approve shortly.

The Declaration of Independence was drafted by a committee which included John Adams and Benjamin Franklin, and the text was written by a delegate from Virginia, Thomas Jefferson, chosen for his masterly prose style. "We hold these truths to be self-evident, that all men are created equal, that all are endowed by their creator with certain unalienable rights, that among these are life, liberty and the pursuit of happiness," it proclaims. It continues with a firm condemnation of King George III: "... the history of the present King of Great Britain is a history of repeated injuries and usurptions, all having in direct object the establishment of an absolute tyranny over these States" and goes on to outline injustices.

The declaration lists some 26 examples of British tyranny which range from the king's obstruction of justice, to the cutting off of American trade with the rest of the world, the waging of war on the colonies and the quartering of armed troops on the colonial peoples. No one can doubt the power and sincerity of this document, least of all the British Parliament which has been "petitioned for redress in the most humble terms" yet "only answered by repeated injury." King George III is seen as "unfit to be the ruler of a free people."

And as the bells ring out in this town tonight and the king's statues are toppled to the ground, John Adams sums up the feeling of the people about this first day. "It ought to be solemnized with pomp and parade, with shows, games, sports, guns, bells, bonfires, and illuminations, from one end of this continent to the other, from this day forward for ever more," he said.

Parisian Mob Storms the Bastille

Paris, 14 July 1789

The people of Paris today stormed the Bastille, the grim prison which was the symbol of absolute monarchy. The dramas started at dawn with the looting of another Parisian prison, Invalides, by the mob in search of arms to fight an expected attack by soldiers loyal to the king.

The mob found 32 000 rifles, but no ammunition. A rumour spread that ammunition was stored at the Bastille. The mob rushed there.

The prison was armed with cannon and guarded by 80 soldiers unfit for front-line duty reinforced by 30 Swiss Guards. The crowd, many of them furniture makers armed with their tools, milled around, frightened by the cannons.

A message was sent to the revoluntionary Assembly which despatched a delegation to negotiate with the Bastille's governor, Bernard de Launay. He promptly invited the envoys into the prison for lunch. When they did not return the mob became angry, believing they had been arrested.

A second delegation was then sent in, only to re-emerge to say that the governor refused to surrender. The spokesperson added, however, that the cannon were unloaded and that de Launay had promised not to fire if they did not attack. But by now the crowd was in no mood to listen to reason.

The cry went up: "We want the Bastille! Down with the army!" The army in fact showed no desire to intervene, withdrawing to the Champ de Mars. Suddenly a group of youths climbed on to a perfumier's shop built against the prison wall and dropped into the courtyard. They let the draw-bridge fall with a crash, killing one of the crowd. The mob rushed into the courtyard. There was a volley of shots. People fell. A howl of rage went up and the fire was returned.

The fighting raged on into the afternoon until cannon were dragged through the streets to blow down the gates. De Launay surrendered before they could fire; his severed head was later paraded by the mob. There were only seven prisoners in the whole prison, but that was unimportant. An ancient symbol of royal tyranny had fallen.

Bolsheviks Stage Bloodless Coup

Petrograd, 7 November 1917

A mantelpiece clock in the Winter Palace stopped at 10 minutes past two this morning. That was the moment when a party of "Red Guards," followed by an unruly mob, burst into the room and seized members of the provisional government. The cabinet ministers narrowly escaped being lynched by the mob before they were carted off to the Peter and Paul fortress. The total casualties in this seizure of power by a group of political conspirators known as Bolsheviks was three officer cadets wounded.

The leader of the Bolsheviks is a former law student, Vladimir Lenin, who only a few months ago was living in exile in Switzerland, virtually unknown outside the unholy circle of police agents and revolutionary visionaries. But the Germans knew him and sent him back to Russia in a sealed train: a troublemaker who they hoped would knock his country out of the war. That was after the February Revolution, when liberals and moderate socialists finally got rid of tsarist autocracy following months of military defeats.

In the euphoria of those days there was no sympathy for the Bolsheviks, and Lenin fled to Finland to escape arrest. But the people were war-weary and hungry, and the provisional government, led by Alexander Kerensky, had only rhetoric to offer.

The coup was masterminded by Leon Trotsky, once Lenin's bitter critic but now his closest comrade. Trotsky got the Petrograd Soviet, or revolutionary assembly, to vote for action, and sent armed squads to take railway stations, the telephone exchange and other key points. When the cruiser *Aurora* came up the Neva River and fired a blank shell outside the Winter Palace, it was pretty well all over.

SIMON BOLÍVAR DREAMS OF SOUTH AMERICAN LIBERATION

by Kenneth and Valerie McLeish

Inspired by revolutionary ideas and events in Europe and America, Simon Bolívar dedicated his life to freedom. He vowed to liberate South America from Spanish rule and create independent countries—and his success was amazing.

Bolívar was born in Caracas, Venezuela, in 1783. As a young man, he went to Europe, where he was influenced by the ideas of Jean-Jacques Rousseau and by the French Revolution. He vowed to free Venezuela from Spanish rule. When the Venezuelan revolution against Spain broke out in 1810, Bolívar joined a group of patriots. They seized the city of Caracas and proclaimed Venezuela's independence, but in 1812 the Spanish regained Caracas. Bolívar recaptured the city in 1813, but two years later, in 1815, the Spanish overpowered him and his patriots once again. Bolívar was forced into exile in Haiti. From there he led an invasion of Venezuela in 1816, where he captured the city of Angostura (now Ciudad Bolívar).

In 1819, Bolívar led his patriot army across the freezing, snow-covered Andes Mountains into Colombia. They took the Spanish there completely by surprise and defeated them at Boyacá, making Colombia independent. The new republic of Gran Colombia was proclaimed, and Bolívar was made its president. The republic included what are now Colombia and Venezuela. (Panama joined it in 1821 and Ecuador in 1822.) Bolívar returned to Caracas in 1821 and liberated Venezuela. Ecuador was taken from the Spanish in 1822.

Bolívar next turned to Peru. He met with the Argentine liberator José de San Martin at Guayaquil. San Martín agreed to allow Bolívar and his army to be the liberators of Peru. The next year part of Peru was renamed Bolivia in Bolívar's honour.

Then Bolívar's dream of a united Spanish America began to come apart. The countries of Gran Colombia wanted more independence for themselves. Revolts broke out. In 1828, Bolívar tried to save Gran Colombia by declaring himself dictator. But the very next night he barely managed to escape an assassination attempt. The collapse of his republic continued. Venezuela and Ecuador seceded. In 1830, ill, tired, and discouraged, Bolívar resigned as president of Gran Colombia. Soon after that he died, poor and bitterly disappointed. But today Bolívar is regarded as one of South America's greatest heroes.

AFRICAN-AMERICANS FIGHT TO ABOLISH SLAVERY

by Howard Smead

In the long struggle to eliminate slavery in the southern United States, the slaves themselves played an important part. So did black abolitionists such as Harriet Tubman and Frederick Douglass. Here are some of their stories.

Once the booming cotton industry reinforced slavery in the South, blacks staged just four revolts, only two of which gained any momentum. The first occurred in 1800 in Richmond, Virginia, under the leadership of a slave name Gabriel Prosser. Gabriel's Revolt was secretly planned for months. It involved 1000 slaves, all of whom had organized into a small fighting force, armed with guns, pikes, scythes, and bayonets. The rebel slaves met about 10 km outside of Richmond, intending to capture the city and to occupy it until the state legislature guaranteed that slavery would be outlawed. The plan was foiled when a slave betrayed the plot to authorities. Virginia governor James Monroe led the local militia out to meet the slaves and to turn them back. No battle ensued, but the leaders of the uprising, including Gabriel Prosser, were arrested and executed.

In 1811 the least-known but largest slave revolt in American history took place in St. John-the-Baptist Parish, Louisiana, just outside New Orleans. The revolt included some 500 slaves who had been brought to Louisiana by their French colonial masters, who were themselves refugees from the Haitian slave revolt. After arriving in North America, these slaves escaped, armed themselves, and marched on New Orleans with drums beating and flags flying. The militia, much better armed, rode out to meet them and attacked. Although the slaves fought bravely, they had no chance of winning and the militia triumphed.

Eleven years later in Charleston, South Carolina, Denmark Vesey, a slave who had purchased his own freedom, organized a plot among slaves to seize the city and ransom it in exchange for an end to slavery. Vesey devised a complex scheme to kidnap government leaders. On the eve of the revolt, however, a slave disclosed the plot to whites, and Vesey and his conspirators were arrested. South Carolina authorities apprehended 131 slaves in all and hanged 37, including Vesey.

The best-known slave revolt in the history of the United States occurred in 1831 in Southampton, Virginia. It was led by a plantation head slave named Nat Turner, who rose up in revolt with other slaves and killed his master and the master's family. These slayings initiated a wholesale slave insurrection that progressed from one plantation to another as slaves murdered their owners and liberated each other. Turner's uprising led to the deaths of about 60 whites and included among its participants approximately 70 slaves. The rampage was halted when federal and state troops crushed the rebellion and captured and executed Turner.

Slave revolts were just one means by which slaves in the South offered resistance to their bondage. Because outright rebellion posed great dangers for them, slaves employed more subtle means of protest. For example, slaves would covertly and purposely break plantation machinery or would set fire to a barn—acts that disrupted the daily life of the plantation and thereby lightened their own burden.

The slaves' prime target was the overseer. When this hated figure drove slaves especially hard or otherwise mistreated them, they sometimes resorted to outright murder. More often, slaves tried to sabotage the overseer, either by getting the overseer drunk on corn liquor, a staple in the slave quarters, or by informing the master, through one of the house servants, that the overseer had committed an indiscretion.

When all else failed, slaves ran away. Between 200 and 300 slaves escaped every year, most of them from the upper South and the border states.

In all, some 60 000 slaves escaped to free territory. They usually journeyed north via one of two routes: through eastern Maryland into Delaware and Pennsylvania or through western Maryland and across the Mason-Dixon Line—the border between Pennsylvania, a free state, and Maryland, a slaveholding state—into central Pennsylvania. Sometimes slaves followed trails farther west, such as those along the Mississippi or Ohio rivers, that led them north.

The vast majority of slaves ended their flight in Canada, where slavery had been outlawed by the mother country, England. Canada was much more enlightened about slavery than the United States. Canadian law not only admitted runaways into the country; it also denied entry to professional slave catchers—poor whites known as "patty rollers"—sent to track the blacks down.

The United States, in contrast, granted federal assistance to slave owners trying to recover their slaves. In 1793 Congress passed the Fugitive Slave Law, which made it a criminal offence for a citizen to harbour a fugitive slave or to prevent his or her arrest. A second piece of legislation—the Fugitive Slave Act of 1850—increased sanctions against aiding runaway slaves. Nowhere in the United States, not even in the antislavery North, could a runaway slave be completely safe from capture and re-enslavement.

Slave-state legislatures feared political pressure from antislavery groups would seriously damage the "peculiar institution," a euphemism used by some apologists for slavery. By 1860 the slave codes had become so tyrannical that it was nearly impossible even for willing masters to *manumit*, or free from bondage, their own slaves. The only recourse the master had was to obtain passage of a special act by the state legislature, a process that cost time and money.

In any case, few slaves relied on the kindness of masters. Instead they plotted their own journey to freedom. Many who succeeded did so by escaping along a series of trails and paths collectively known as the Underground Railroad. This secret route from the South to the North was led by "conductors," brave men and women who sneaked into slave territory to guide runaway slaves out of bondage. The most famous conductor was Harriet Tubman. She had escaped from a Maryland plantation in 1849 and at great risk to her own safety—a bounty had been put on her head—returned to the South as many as 19 times to lead slaves on the Underground Railroad. She alone escorted 600 slaves to freedom, including her sister, both her children, and her mother and father.

Tubman plotted these escapes down to the smallest detail. She preferred to start her journeys on a Saturday night because owners could not print newspaper announcements of runaways until Monday morning, and the time in between gave her a headstart. Tubman had great sympathy for enslaved blacks, but none for cowards. If one of her party lost his or her nerve, Tubman pulled out the pistol she always carried and then threatened to kill the runaway with the words "live free or die." She also brought along a small vial of tincture of opium, a sedative for crying babies, when slave catchers lurked nearby.

Harriet Tubman was just one of many men and women known as abolitionists because they worked to abolish slavery. They viewed the peculiar institution as immoral and unchristian and could not comprehend how Americans, who were steeped in the tenets of their Declaration of Independence, could sanction the enslavement of human beings in their midst. The abolitionist movement attracted members of both races, including the prominent journalist William Lloyd Garrison, who published the *Liberator*, the leading antislavery newspaper of the day.

The vast majority of abolitionists, however, were blacks. Many made their home in the North and worked as clergymen. Others, like Frederick Douglass, an escaped slave who held several government-appointed posts after the Civil War, published abolitionist newspapers such as the *North Star*, named after the star that guided conductors on the Underground Railroad. Douglass used this journal to publicize the antislavery cause and to promote the works of black writers such as Phillis Wheatley, a poet who lived at the time of the American Revolution.

Some abolitionists grew so disillusioned with

the United States that they simply left the country. Reverend Alexander Crummell and Edward Wilmot Blyden founded a colony of freed American blacks in Liberia, a country on the coast of West Africa. Martin R. Delany, a black physician, led an effort to establish a colony in Africa at the bend of the Niger River. He returned to the United States in 1865 and led black troops who fought in the Union army. Like other abolitionists, he threw himself wholeheartedly into the violent struggle over slavery between Northern and Southern states, a bloody conflict that would claim the lives of more than 500 000 soldiers and countless civilians, known to history as the Civil War.

▲▼▶▼▶▲▼▶▼▶▲▼▶▼▶▲▼▶▼▶

The personal stories of many former slaves have been passed down from generation to generation. Here's one story.

"Granma used to tell this story to everybody that would listen, and I expect I heard it a hundred times. Granma say she was hired out to the Randolphs during the war. One day while she was weeding corn another slave, Mamie Tolliver, come up to her and whispered, "Sarah, they tell me that

Massa Lincoln done set all us slaves free."

Granma say, "Is that so?" and she dropped her hoe and run all the way to the Thacker's place—seven miles [11 km] it was—and run to ol' missus and looked at her real hard. Then she yelled, "I'm free! Yes, I'm free! Ain't got to work for you no more. You can't put me in your pocket now!"

Granma say Missus Thacker started boo-hooing and threw her apron over her face and run in the house. Granma knew it was true then."

Betty Jones
The Negro in Virginia

CHECKING OUT ME HISTORY

Dem tell me
Dem tell me
Wha dem want fo tell me

Bandage up me eye with me own history
Blind me to me own identity

Dem tell me bout 1066 and all dat
Dem tell me bout Dick Whittington and he cat
But Toussaint L'Ouverture[1]
no dem never tell me bout dat

Toussaint
a slave
with vision
lick back
Napoleon
battalion
and first Black

Republic born
Toussaint de thorn
to de French
Toussaint de beacon
of de Haitian Revolution

Dem tell me bout de man who discover de balloon
and de cow who jump over de moon

Dem tell me bout de dish run away with de spoon
but dem never tell me bout Nanny[2] de maroon

Nanny
see-far woman
of mountain dream
fire-woman struggle
hopeful stream
to freedom river

Dem tell me bout Lord Nelson and Waterloo
but dem never tell me bout Shaka de great Zulu
Dem tell me bout Columbus and 1492
but what happen to de Caribs[3] and de Arawaks[4] too

Dem tell me bout Florence Nightingale and she
lamp
and how Robin Hood used to camp
Dem tell me bout old King Cole was a merry ole
soul
but dem never tell me bout Mary Seacole[5]

From Jamaica
she travel far
to the Crimean War

she volunteer to go
and even when de British said no
she still brave the Russian snow
a healing star
among the wounded
a yellow sunrise
to the dying

Dem tell me
Dem tell me wha dem want fo tell me
By now I checking out me own history
I carving out me identity.

John Agard

1. **Toussaint L'Ouverture:** a slave who led an army that defeated forces sent by Napoleon
2. **Nanny:** a national heroine of Jamaica who led runaway slaves to establish a free settlement in the hills of Jamaica
3. **Caribs:** Amerindian tribe from whom the Caribbean got its name
4. **Arawaks:** Amerindian people of the Greater Antilles and South America
5. **Mary Seacole:** Jamaican nurse who put her skills to use in the Crimean War (1853–6) but did not receive the acclaim that Florence Nightingale did

SITTING BULL TRIUMPHS AT LITTLE BIGHORN

by Kenneth and Valerie McLeish

Often called Custer's Last Stand, the battle near Little Bighorn River (in what is now the state of Montana) was an astounding victory for the Sioux. Historians are still debating what mistakes the American military made. But everyone agrees that it was the great Chief Sitting Bull who inspired his Sioux warriors to fight the battle for their lives and land. The battle between Sitting Bull and Custer also symbolizes a deadly clash between two cultures and ways of life.

Sitting Bull (1834(?)–1890)
Sioux Chief

Sitting Bull was born in South Dakota. As a child, he was called Hunkesni, a Sioux word for slow. He earned the name Sitting Bull after showing great courage in a fight against the Crow. It was a name which his father chose for him.

Sitting Bull became a medicine man. A year

before the battle for the Little Bighorn, he received a vision that the Native people would triumph over their enemies. He was the leading medicine man in the preparations for the battle which fell on June 25, 1876. Before the battle, he led a sun dance. He inspired the Native people to fight to kill, not just to show off their courage in battle, or else they would lose their lands to the white people. This unexpected, new fierce way of fighting helped lead to the total defeat of General Custer and his soldiers. After the battle, Sitting Bull and his followers were driven up into Canada. In 1881 Sitting Bull returned to the United States where he was held at Fort Randall in South Dakota for two years. He then lived on the Standing Rock Reservation, where in 1890 he helped to start the Ghost Dance. Fearing another Native uprising, the government sent police to arrest Sitting Bull. Both Sitting Bull and his son were killed in the process.

George Armstrong Custer (1839–1876)
United States Army officer

Custer attended the United States Military Academy at West Point, in New York State. He graduated in 1861, at the bottom of his class. But he soon proved to be a very able soldier. The Civil War had just begun, and Custer fought bravely in many famous cavalry battles. Before the war was over, he had become the Union Army's youngest brigadier general, at only 23. Two years later, he was made a major general. After the war, Custer was dropped to the rank of captain, and when he was assigned to the Seventh Cavalry in 1866 it was as a lieutenant colonel. He commanded the regiment until his death.

In 1876, Custer and his troops were assigned to assist in a campaign under General Alfred H. Terry against the Sioux and Cheyenne. In June 1876 the United States' forces reached what is now southern Montana. General Terry divided his troops into two groups. Custer's group was to approach the Native encampment from the south, near the Little Bighorn River, and get into position to attack when Terry's forces arrived.

On June 25, Custer's scouts found the Native encampment. There were thousands of warriors in the camp, led by Crazy Horse, Gall, and Sitting Bull. But because many of the Natives were hidden in nearby ravines, Custer's scouts guessed that they numbered only about 1000. Custer decided that his troops could easily defeat such a small group on their own without waiting for the rest of the U.S. force. He split his regiment into three groups. One, under Captain Frederick Benteen, was sent to keep the Natives from escaping to the south. Major Marcus Reno was sent across the river to attack. Custer took about 200 men and headed north to charge into the Native camp. The battle lasted less than an hour. Custer's group was quickly surrounded, and every man was killed. Benteen and Reno managed to lead what was left of their soldiers to safety in the hills to wait for Terry and the main U.S. force. The Natives broke camp and left the area.

The battle, which became known as "Custer's Last Stand," is still being argued about by historians and others.

Some believe Custer was wrong for not waiting to attack until Terry's forces had arrived. Some say Reno's men could have rescued Custer's group if they had remained in the battle. Others argue that General Terry should have known how many Natives were in the encampment.

What really happened will probably never be known.

A people without history is like wind on the buffalo grass.

SIOUX PROVERB

CAMPAIGNERS FOR WOMEN'S RIGHTS

In the United States, Susan B. Anthony campaigned so that women could have the right to vote. In Canada, Emily Murphy campaigned for women to become legal "persons." Along with many others, these two have helped to make women and men equal citizens in our countries.

Susan Brownell Anthony (1820–1906)

from Great Lives

Susan Anthony was one of the leaders of the campaign for women's rights in the United States during the second half of the 19th century. Early in life she petitioned for the abolition of slavery, and she believed that women, as well as slaves, should be granted the same legal rights as men. In 1854 Anthony collected 6000 signatures on a petition which asked that women be given the vote, that they be allowed to keep any money they earned, and that they be able to keep their children if they were divorced. This petition, followed by several more, led to some reforms of the laws of New York State.

After the Civil War, when slaves were freed and allowed to vote, women also expected to be granted a vote. This did not happen, and in 1869 Susan Anthony and Elizabeth Cady Stanton (1815–1902) formed the National Women's Suffrage Association to campaign for votes for women. Although the Association was large and energetic in its campaigns, women did not gain the vote during Anthony's lifetime. She also lectured on temperance (abstaining from alcohol) and slavery. She retired in 1900.

Emily Murphy (1868–1933)

by Janet Lunn and Christopher Moore

Emily Murphy was a writer, reformer, and politician at a time when few Canadian women had even one of those occupations. She was born in Ontario in 1868, and moved to Edmonton, Alberta, in 1903, with her husband, an Anglican minister. Emily Murphy wrote popular books under the pen name "Janey Canuck." She worked for women's causes, and she was appointed police magistrate for Edmonton—the first woman in the British Commonwealth to be named a judge.

On her first day on the magistrate's bench, a defence lawyer challenged her. As a woman, he said, she had no right to sit as a judge, since a woman was not legally a person. Judge Murphy and four other women, including writer Nellie McClung, spent 10 years fighting the "Persons Case." In 1928, after the Supreme Court of Canada agreed that women were not legally "persons," the women appealed to England. In 1929 the British Privy Council declared that the ruling was "a relic of days more barbarous than ours," and women were finally recognized as persons.

Time Capsule
HOW TWO WORLD WARS BEGAN

from *Chronicle of the World*

The 20th century has seen the biggest wars in history. World War I (1914–1918) was fought in Europe and shocked people with its senseless slaughter. World War II (1939–1945) began in Europe but spread to include America and Japan. Here is an account of how these wars began.

Archduke's murder unsettles Europe

Sarajevo, Bosnia, 28 June 1914

Archduke Franz Ferdinand, the heir to the Austro-Hungarian empire, and his wife, the duchess of Hohenburg, were assassinated here today by a Serbian nationalist. It was the 14th anniversary of their marriage.

The killer, Gavril Principal, darted out of the crowd as the car carrying the royal couple slowed to change direction. His first bullet struck the archduke in the neck, and the second hit the duchess who had flung herself in front of her husband. The duchess died almost immediately, the archduke 10 minutes later. The murders were evidently part of a concerted plot. Earlier, the couple were on the way to the town hall of this capital of Bosnia when a bomb was thrown into their car. The archduke picked it up and threw it into the road where it exploded, wounding those in a following car.

The implications of this outrage are dangerous in the extreme. The killer, seized by the police, has told them that he wanted to take revenge for the oppression of the Serbian people. He is believed to have been helped by a secret society of Serbian officers known as the "Black Hand." There can be no doubt that the Austrians will make drastic demands on what the Austrian foreign minister, Count von Berchtold, calls the "Serbian wasp's nest." But the Serbs, backed by Russia, are in no mood to be bullied by the Austrians.

The assassination of the Archduke was the spark that set off the First World War. A month later, Austria-Hungary declared war on Serbia.

By August 5, all the great European nations were at war except Italy. On one side were the Allies—Britain, France, and Russia (who supported Serbia). Opposing them were the Central Powers—Germany and Austria-Hungary.

Europe is again at war

London, 30 September 1939

Poland lies shattered, partitioned yet again by her more powerful neighbours. As Polish forces were reeling under the hammer blows of the *Wehrmacht,* the German armed forces, Soviet Union chief minister Joseph Stalin sent Red Army troops to occupy eastern Poland. The treacherous significance of the Nazi-Soviet Pact thus became clear.

Soon after dawn on 1 September, 1.25 million German troops, with six armoured divisions and eight motorized divisions, swept into Poland. The *Luftwaffe,* the German airforce, knocked out the Polish railway system and shot the air force out of the sky. By day three—when Britain and France declared war—the Germans had cut the Polish Corridor and by day eight were at the gates of Warsaw. The city endured two weeks of terror bombing before surrendering.

An estimated 60 000 Poles have been killed, 200 000 wounded and 700 000 taken prisoner. The Polish government has fled to Romania. Hitler has proved that the static trench warfare of 1914–18 is a thing of the past. The English language has acquired a new and terrifying word—*blitzkrieg,* meaning lightning war. In London, after some uncertainty, the British Government declared war on Sunday, 3 September 11 a.m. The French followed at 5 p.m. A joint statement said the two governments would avoid bombing civilians. In Washington, U.S. President Roosevelt announced

United States neutrality, ordering an embargo on the shipment of arms to countries at war.

USA joins the Allies

Pearl Harbor, 7 December 1941

Soon after dawn today, wave after wave of Japanese warplanes began to bomb America's major Pacific base. Pearl Harbor, near Honolulu, Hawaii, was taken entirely by surprise and within two hours the Japanese had destroyed five battleships, 14 smaller craft, and 200 aircraft. At least 2400 people, many of them civilians, were killed. Although the U.S. Navy has suffered a major disaster, Japan's bombers failed to find and hit America's all-important aircraft carriers, both of which were away on manoeuvres.

However, Japanese planes have attacked U.S. bases in the Philippines, on Wake Island and Guam in the middle of the Pacific. The Japanese had obviously planned the operation carefully. Twelve days ago, six aircraft-carriers left the Kurile Islands in total secrecy and headed for Honolulu. The first bombs fell even as Japanese diplomats were meeting with the United States Government in Washington. Congress will meet to declare war in emergency session tomorrow—to the infinite relief of Britain.

UPRISING IN THE WARSAW GHETTO

by R. Conrad Stein

Before World War II, Warsaw, Poland, had the largest Jewish population of any European city. Within four years, there were almost no Jews remaining in the capital. This is the story of the Warsaw Ghetto.

World War II in Europe is sometimes called "the war against the Jews." Hatred of Jewish people was basic to Nazi philosophy. Adolf Hitler and the Nazis rose to power in the 1930s largely because they were able to convince the German people that the Jews were responsible for the misfortunes suffered by Germany after World War I. As the war progressed, Jews in territory occupied by the Nazis were systematically murdered.

In eastern Europe, and especially in Poland, the slaughter of Jews reached appalling proportions. It is estimated that fully 90 percent of all Polish Jews failed to survive World War II. Even German Jews fared better than Polish Jews. But in

Poland, small pockets of Jewish people fought back. Their most heroic struggle occurred in the Warsaw Ghetto.

Before the war, Warsaw had the largest Jewish population of any European city. Some 400 000 Jewish people lived there. After the German victory in 1939, workers built walls and strung rows of barbed wire around a slum area that measured about 100 square blocks. All non-Jews were ordered to vacate the section. Warsaw's 400 000 Jews, together with about 100 000 other Jews who lived in the countryside, were then herded into the compound. Thus the Warsaw Ghetto was born.

The people within the ghetto's walls were dependent entirely on the Germans for food. The Germans gave the ghetto people only bread and potatoes to eat. Often the bread was mouldy and the potatoes rancid. Hunger gnawed at everyone's insides. "My belly talks, shouts, and drives me mad," wrote one man. A reporter noted that "hunger, sickness, and want are [the people's] constant companions, and death is the only visitor in their homes."

The winter of 1940–41 was the coldest the people of Warsaw could remember. Yet the German authorities allowed no fuel to be shipped into the ghetto. Lumps of coal became so scarce they were called "black pearls." Families broke up precious articles of furniture and burned them in order to enjoy a few moments of warmth. Many

Jews had no coats or warm shoes. In his journal, ghetto leader Emmanuel Ringelblum wrote: "The most fearsome sight is that of freezing children standing, weeping in the streets with bare feet, bare knees, and torn clothing."

Spring triggered a cultural explosion that was astonishing after the bitterness of the winter. Newspapers printed on hand-operated presses circulated in the ghetto. People donated books to form neighbourhood libraries. Concerts were given on the streets. Even a few movies were smuggled in from the outside.

The Jews, who had revered scholarship for centuries, set up secret classrooms in basements. Schools were strictly forbidden by the Germans. A teacher named Chaim Kaplan wrote, "Jewish children learn in secret. In time of danger [they] hide their books and notebooks between their trousers and their stomachs, then button their jackets and coats."

The gentler spring weather also aided the work of the food smugglers. These smugglers, many of whom were children, became heroes of the ghetto. At night they sneaked through holes in the walls or crawled under barbed wire to get to the streets of greater Warsaw. Many of those discovered by German guards were shot on sight. On the streets the smugglers bought, traded for, or stole food. Then, with sacks bulging with bread and tins of fish, they crept back into the ghetto. A popular song was written to honour them:

Over the wall, through holes, and past the
guard,
Through the wires, ruins, and fence,
Plucky, hungry, and determined,
I sneak through, dart like a cat.

In 1941, German overlords announced the start of a "resettlement" program. The Jews were told that large numbers of them were to be transferred to work camps in the east. One of the largest of the camps was at the Polish town of Treblinka, a short train ride from Warsaw. The Nazis claimed that those going to the camps would eat well and be put to work in factories and in farmers' fields.

Starting in July, each day 5000 people were marched through the streets toward the train station. The Germans gave the deportees a generous supply of food. Each marcher clung to three loaves of fresh bread and several tins of marmalade presented to him or her by German guards. This was more food than most ghetto dwellers had seen in months. Many of the Jews who saw their neighbours carrying so much bread volunteered to go to the work camps.

Rumours leaked into the ghetto that Treblinka was really a death camp, but most Jews refused to listen to such improbable stories. They argued that in the 20th century no nation would kill people just because of the religion they practised.

Then, bit by bit, shocking and unbelievable

news came to Warsaw through the secret network of messengers that connected the ghettos of Poland. Treblinka was not a work camp at all. It was instead a death station. The rumours were grimly confirmed. Resettlement meant death.

Late in 1942, a small band of ghetto rebels decided to rise up against the Germans. By that time, "resettlement," starvation, and disease had reduced the Warsaw Ghetto's population from 500 000 to less than 100 000. The leaders of the ghetto rebellion were mostly young, idealistic men and women. They had no illusions about achieving victory in a military sense. The rebels wanted only to give some meaning to their deaths. As one of them wrote in his diary: "We have nothing to expect but a choice of two kinds of death.... When we fight it will have to be to the last."

The ghetto fighters needed weapons. Teams of crafty young smugglers were sent into the streets to buy or trade for pistols, bullets, and sticks of dynamite. In basement workshops the rebels fashioned crude bombs from sawed-off water pipes. They sharpened kitchen knives to a fine edge, and made clubs of steel rods.

In January, 1943, the ghetto fighters struck. They deposed the hated Jewish police force. They proclaimed that the ghetto was now in their hands. At first, the German guards, accustomed to no resistance, were too astonished to act. Once in power, the rebels distributed leaflets proclaiming, "Jews! Do not resign yourselves to death! Defend yourselves! Grab an axe, an iron bar, or a knife! Let them take you this way if they can."

The Nazis refused to believe that a few hot-headed young Jews could defy their authority. So, when the shock wore off, they marched as usual into the walled community seeking their quota of deportees. But they were greeted by the fury of a bold and determined guerrilla force.

The Jews waged a bloody, street-by-street, hit-and-run campaign. The ghetto fighters knew every centimetre of the tangle of gangways and back alleys that sprawled through their compound. They lashed out at the Germans, firing their pistols and hurling their homemade bombs. Then they melted out of sight behind the buildings. Again and again the ghetto fighters struck and disappeared. The Germans were bewildered by this type of battle.

The January battles lasted four days. The ghetto fighters killed 20 Germans and wounded 50 more. Their own losses were frightful. But, miraculously, the ferocious offensive drove the Nazi guards out of the ghetto.

The Jewish victory stunned the Nazis. They feared that the Warsaw rebellion would spread to other ghettos in eastern Europe. For the next three months, the Germans surrounded the Warsaw Ghetto and tried to persuade the rebels to lay down their arms. There were no takers.

Enraged, the Germans called on their army. A ruthless general named Jürgen Stroop was given the task of destroying resistance in the ghetto. After the war, Stroop was one of many German generals convicted of war crimes. He was sentenced to death and was hanged on September 8, 1951.

Initially, the well-equipped Germans suffered dozens of defeats at the hands of the Jews. "What we have lived through after two days of defence defies description in words," wrote ghetto commander Mordecai Anielewicz. "We must realize that what has happened exceeds our most audacious dreams.... I have the feeling that what we have dared is of great significance." But the ghetto fighters were fighting a war that was impossible to win. Inside their compound they had no reserves. No bullet they fired, no crumb they ate, no drop of water they drank could be replaced.

After a week of street fighting, General Stroop switched tactics. He moved up heavy guns and pounded the ghetto with around-the-clock artillery bombardment. Finally, the general ordered flamethrower teams to burn down the ghetto.

Even in the face of flames the Jews refused to give up. Their stubborn resistance astonished General Stroop. In his report to Berlin he wrote: "The Jews stayed in the burning buildings until, because of the fear of being burned alive, they jumped down from the upper storeys.... With their bones broken they still tried to crawl across the street into buildings which had not yet been set on fire.... Despite the danger of being burned alive the Jews and bandits often preferred to return into the flames rather than risk being caught by us."

No amount of human courage could defy the surging wall of flames or the shells the Germans poured into the ghetto. Ghetto dwellers died by the thousands. When the situation proved hopeless, many Jews surrendered and were sent to Treblinka.

On May 16, 1943, General Stroop wrote his last daily battle report: "The former Jewish quarter of Warsaw is no longer in existence. The large-scale action was terminated at 20:15 hours by blowing up the Warsaw Synagogue.... Total number of Jews dealt with: 56,065, including both Jews caught and Jews whose extermination can be proved."

The ghetto uprising was over, and with it the Jewish community of Warsaw died. Once the most Jewish city in Europe, Warsaw now had no significant Jewish element remaining. The Polish capital's Jewish population had either been put to death, imprisoned, or had died in the fighting. The scant few Jews remaining in the city hid in sewers or in the homes of Polish friends.

But the courage of Warsaw's Jews never died. They faced enslavement with dignity and death with bravery.

AN ATOMIC BOMB TARGETS HIROSHIMA

by Michael O'Neal

In 1941, Japanese planes bombed the American naval fleet at Pearl Harbor, Hawaii. This attack brought the United States into World War II and spurred on their decision to create the most powerful bomb the world had ever seen.

Early in the morning of August 6, 1945, air raid sirens sounded throughout the city of Hiroshima, Japan. Residents took cover, but nothing happened. This was not the first time that an expected attack by American bombers had failed to occur. So the people of Hiroshima went about their morning's business.

When air raid sirens sounded again shortly after eight o'clock, many people in the city remained unconcerned, thinking that it was just another false alarm. For some people, work in the factories had just started. Homemakers were planning their day's errands, and school for most of the city's children had just begun. The few people who were outdoors, or who happened to be looking out a window, were pleased to see a parachute drifting slowly to earth—the usual sign that an American bomber had been hit by anti-aircraft fire, forcing its pilot to parachute to safety.

But what most of these people never learned was that dangling from the end of this parachute was an atomic bomb—the first bomb of this type that had ever been used in warfare. At an altitude of just under 610 m, the bomb detonated. With a flash of light, Hiroshima lay in ruins, blasted beyond recognition. Destruction on this scale had never been seen in war—and has never been seen since. In seconds, an area 1.5 km across was utterly destroyed. Not a single building was left even partially standing as a result of the explosion—an explosion whose force was that of over 10 million kg of dynamite.

The destructive effects of the bomb did not stop with the initial blast. Within moments a tremendous firestorm began to consume everything within hundreds of metres of the blast. This firestorm created a ball of heat so intense that fires sprang up as far as three kilometres from the centre of the explosion. The intense heat carried soot and debris skyward, creating the "mushroom cloud" characteristic of atomic explosions. By evening an ashy "black rain" was falling on the city, leaving ugly stains on everything it touched.

Overshadowing the complete destruction of

the city was the loss of human life. Eighty-thousand people were killed almost instantly by the initial blast. Another 100 000 were seriously injured, many of them badly burned. Thousands of survivors wandered about the devastated city, dazed, searching for friends and relatives and seeking medical help for their injuries. What the survivors did not know was that their bodies had been invaded by radioactivity. For days, months, and even years, this radioactivity would cause a legacy of stillbirths, birth defects, cancer, and other diseases. Harder to measure was the sense of loss and despair among the survivors, leading many to believe that those who had been quickly killed were the lucky ones.

Three days later the city of Nagasaki met a similar fate, at a cost of over 40 000 lives. Faced with the savage destructiveness of the atomic bomb, the Japanese government—at war with the United States since 1941—surrendered, bringing World War II to an end. The atomic bomb had done what was promised, but on a scale that no one had ever imagined.

Rest in peace. The mistake shall not be repeated.

INSCRIPTION ON MEMORIAL TO JAPAN'S WAR DEAD

PEACE PARK, HIROSHIMA

NEIL ARMSTRONG LANDS ON THE MOON

from *Great Lives*

In the years following the end of the Second World War in 1945, Russia and the United States became the world's two superpowers. Besides continuing the arms race by building nuclear weapons, they competed to be the first to conquer space. Millions of people were thrilled by the televised images of satellites and astronauts and spacecraft. But most exciting to many was the landing of the first person on the Moon.

The short history of space flight with astronauts on board began on April 12, 1961, when a Soviet cosmonaut, Yuri Gagarin, made a single successful orbit of the earth in his tiny *Vostok 1* capsule. A few weeks later, President Kennedy officially launched the *Apollo* program, saying that within 10 years America would put a person on the moon and return him or her safely to earth. Remarkably, his words came true: on July 21, 1969,

Neil Armstrong stepped from the *Eagle* lunar landing craft onto the moon's surface and transmitted the words "That's one small step for man, one giant leap for mankind" back to earth.

The *Apollo 11* flight that delivered Armstrong and his companions, Buzz Aldrin and Michael Collins, to the moon was the result of rapid advances in science and technology, as well as the expenditure of billions of dollars. In 1965 and 1966 10 *Gemini* missions with astronauts aboard proved that astronauts could live and work in space, and gave both them and the scientists on the ground the opportunity to experiment with equipment and practise different manoeuvres. Meanwhile, engineers developed the giant *Saturn V* rockets, powerful enough to launch the lunar landing craft and send it on its way to the moon. The first craft to travel to the moon was *Apollo 8*, which circled it 10 times at Christmas, 1968.

Apollo 11 was launched the following summer. On July 20, Armstrong and Aldrin crawled from the command module, in orbit around the moon, into the lunar landing vehicle. Collins remained behind, circling above as the two astronauts explored the lunar landscape. The landing was not easy: an error in the craft's computers meant that Armstrong had to juggle the controls to land safely. But once on the ground, he radioed a message back to the controllers waiting in Houston, Texas: "Houston—Tranquility Base here. The Eagle has landed."

The two men spent just a day on the moon's surface. Five more successful *Apollo* missions followed, together with one near disaster. In April 1970 an explosion on board *Apollo 13* put the lives of three astronauts in grave danger. They circled the moon and returned to earth with barely enough oxygen to survive, but eventually made a safe splashdown, in the ocean. The last mission, *Apollo 17*, took place in 1972. The entire program had been a combination of remarkable scientific and technical skill, and the daring of a few people like Neil Armstrong.

HISTORY OF SPACE

by Brenda Ralph Lewis, Philip Steele, and Lynne Williams

1957 *Sputnik I*, the first earth satellite, launched by the USSR.

1959 The USSR launches the space probe *Luna 1* and the USA launches the space probe *Pioneer 4*.

1961 The Soviet Yuri Gagarin becomes the first human to travel in space, when his spacecraft *Vostok 1* is launched.

1962 First Americans in orbit: John Glenn in

February and M. Scott Carpenter in May.

1962 The US satellite *Telstar* launched from Cape Canaveral, Florida, enables transatlantic television to be transmitted.

1962 The USA launches the rocket *Mariner* to explore the planet Venus and the USSR launches *Mars 1* to explore Mars. *Mariner* sends back its first readings in December, after four months.

1963 The Soviet Valentina Tereshkova makes a three-day space flight. She is the first woman to travel in space.

1964 *Ranger VII* takes close-up pictures of the moon's surface.

1965 Soviet cosmonaut Alexei Leonov takes the first space walk (March). First American space walk by Edward White (June).

1966 First successful docking in space by the American *Gemini 8*. Soviet *Lunik IX* makes the first landing on the moon without astronauts on board and sends back pictures of the surface.

1967 First space fatalities: three US astronauts die in fire on *Apollo I* while still on the launch pad. *Mariner V* launched to Mars by USA. Soviet capsule lands on Venus.

1968 *Apollo 8*, first vehicle with astronauts aboard to orbit the moon.

1969 First landing on the moon by astronauts

from American *Apollo 11*, July 21.

1971 Soviets launch first space station, *Salyut I.*

1973 Americans launch space station, *Skylab.*

1975 Link up in space by Soviet *Soyuz* and American *Apollo* spacecraft.

1979 USA launches *Voyager I* to the planet Jupiter.

1981 First flight of the space shuttle *Columbia.* The Canadarm, designed to grasp and repair satellites in space, flew on the second shuttle flight and performed well.

1983 Second space shuttle, *Challenger*, launched by the USA.

1984 Marc Garneau becomes the first Canadian astronaut to enter space on the space shuttle *Challenger.*

1986 *Challenger*, with the first civilian passenger to fly in space on board, blows up after launch, killing all on board.

1992 Canada's first woman astronaut, Roberta Bondar, flew aboard the shuttle *Discovery* and performed scientific experiments.

THE BERLIN WALL CRASHES DOWN

by Robert Darnton

The Berlin Wall was the symbol of the Cold War. Built in August 1961 by the Soviets, it divided East and West Berlin—and symbolized the division of the Communist world from the Western democratic world. It was heavily guarded. Anyone trying to escape over it to the West was shot at and often killed. Then in 1989, the Cold War ended. In a moment of great excitement, Berliners danced on the ruins of the hated Wall. Shortly afterwards, East and West Germany were united.

On the morning of November 10, 1989, when residents of both East and West Berlin woke up wondering whether the first flood through the Wall had been a dream, the West Berlin tabloid *Volksblatt* ran two headlines, shoulder to shoulder, on its front page: "The Wall Is Gone" and "Bonn [capital of West Germany] Demands the

Destruction of the Wall."

Both were right. The Wall is there and it is not there. On November 9, it cut through the heart of Berlin, a jagged wound in the middle of a great city, the Great Divide of the Cold War. On November 10, it had become a dance floor, a picture gallery, a bulletin board, a movie screen, a videocassette, a museum, and, as the woman who cleaned my office put it, "nothing but a heap of stone." The taking of the Wall, like the taking of the Bastille, transformed the world. No wonder that a day later, in Alexanderplatz, East Berlin, one conqueror of the Wall marched in a demonstration with a sign saying simply, "1789–1989." He had helped dismantle the central symbol around which the postwar world had taken shape in the minds of millions.

To witness symbolic transformation on such a scale is a rare opportunity, and it raises many questions. To begin with the most concrete: What happened between November 9 and 12, and what does it mean?

The destruction of the Wall began in the early evening of Thursday, November 9, soon after the first wave of East Berliners, or *Ossis*, as they are called by the West Berliners here, burst upon the West. One Ossi, a young man with a knapsack on his back, somehow hoisted himself up on the Wall directly across from the Brandenburg Gate. He sauntered along the top of it, swinging his arms casually at his sides, a perfect target for the bullets that had felled many other wall jumpers, like Peter Fechter, an 18-year-old construction worker, who was shot and left to bleed to death about a metre in front of Checkpoint Charlie[1], on August 17, 1962. Now 27 years later, a new generation of border guards took aim at a new kind of target and fired—but only with power hoses and without much conviction. The conqueror of the Wall continued his promenade, soaked to the skin, until at last the guards gave up. Then he opened his knapsack and poured the water toward the East, in a gesture that seemed to say, "Goodbye to all that."

A few minutes later, hundreds of people, Ossis and *Wessis* (as the West Berliners are known) alike, were on the Wall, embracing, dancing, exchanging flowers, drinking wine, helping up new "conquerors",—and chipping away at the Wall itself. By midnight, under a full moon and the glare of spotlights from the watchtowers in no man's land, 1000 figures swarmed over the Wall, hammering, chiseling, wearing its surface away like a colony of army ants. At the bottom, "conquerors" threw stones at its base or went at it with pickaxes. Long slits appeared, and the light showed through from the East, as if through the eyes of a jack-o'-lantern. On the top, at the centre of the tumult, with the Brandenburg Gate looming in the background, one Ossi conducted the destruction with a sickle in one hand and a hammer in the other, the symbols of communism.

By Saturday, November 11, chunks of the

wall were circulating through both Berlins. People exchanged them as souvenirs of what had already taken shape in the collective consciousness as a historical event: the end of the Cold War. A sidewalk entrepreneur sold bits of wall from a table on the Kurfürstendamm, West Berlin's elegant shopping avenue: 20 DM [Deutschemarks, the currency in West Germany] for a piece of the past. At one point, an East Berliner walked by and objected, with a smile on his face: "You can't sell that. It's our Wall. It belongs to us."

1. **Checkpoint Charlie**: the American-controlled side of a border crossing along the Berlin Wall. It became a symbol of freedom during the Cold War.

NELSON MANDELA IS RELEASED FROM PRISON

by Barry Denenberg

Nelson Mandela is black South Africa's most famous leader. Head of the African National Congress (ANC), he was imprisoned by the South African government for almost 30 years, about half of his adult life. During that time, his people never forgot him. After his release, he continued to negotiate with the government for an end to apartheid and equal rights for blacks.

In August 1988, Nelson Mandela was suffering from a bad cough and was having trouble speaking. He was hospitalized with tuberculosis. He might have caught it in his damp cell at Pollsmoor prison, near Cape Town. Or, as some speculated, it might have begun as far back as his hard years imprisoned at the penitentiary on Robben Island. He was in pain and his appearance was shocking.

He was taken to one of the best medical centres in the country. By October his condition had improved. There was a good chance he would recover completely.

Two months later he was moved to a cottage at Victor Verster Prison. Victor Verster was a prison farm with a swimming pool. The government published photographs picturing the comfort Mandela was living in. They were the first photographs released since 1966 on Robben Island.

Mandela lived in a three-bedroom house over 1.5 km away from the main prison building. On Robben Island and in Pollsmoor the companionship of his fellow prisoners had been important. Now, isolated, he was not allowed to leave his compound. He saw only guards. The loneliness was difficult to bear.

During Mandela's illness, high government officials were concerned that he might die while in prison. If that happened they feared the increased violence that was sure to follow—violence they might not be able to contain as they had so far.

News of his illness brought renewed demands for his release.

By now Nelson Mandela had spent more than half his adult life behind bars. He had become the symbol of the movement for black liberation in South Africa. Children who were not yet born when he was jailed cried his name. He stood for freedom to millions who had neither seen nor heard him. The overwhelming majority of black South Africans considered him their leader. Others, white as well as black, realized that only his release could end the crisis that was threatening to destroy their country.

Speculation about Mandela's release increased in the second half of the 1980s. The question became not *if* but *when*. When would the ruling National Party be willing for the first time to talk with black South Africans?

It was rumoured that Mandela was studying Afrikaans, a modified form of the Dutch language used in South Africa, in preparation for the negotiations he hoped would finally come about.

But Nelson Mandela had been offered his freedom before and had refused it.

In January 1985, President P.W. Botha offered to release Mandela. Mandela, Botha stipulated, had to agree to a number of conditions. He had to formally reject violence and agree to live in the Transkei. The Transkei, the place where he was born, was now one of the so-called homelands. Officials of the government said they no longer stood in the way of a free Nelson Mandela; the choice was his.

On Sunday, February 10, 1985, Zindzi Mandela read her father's response to the government's offer. Ten thousand people had gathered at Jabulani amphitheatre in Soweto. The United Democratic Front was honouring Bishop Desmond Tutu, who had been awarded the Nobel Peace Prize the year before. Wearing the yellow T-shirt of the UDF, Zindzi, now 25, told the audience:

My father and his comrades wish to make this statement to you the people, first.... My father says, "I am surprised at the conditions that the government wants to impose on me! It was only when all other forms of resistance were no longer open to us that we turned to armed struggle....

"I cherish my own freedom dearly but I care even more for your freedom. Too many have died since I went to prison. Too many have suffered for the love of freedom. I owe it to their widows, to their orphans, to their mothers, and to their fathers who have grieved and wept for them. Not only I have suffered during these lonely wasted years. I am not less life-loving than you are. But I cannot sell my birthright nor am I prepared to sell the birthright of the people to be free.... What freedom am I being offered while the organization of the people remains banned? What freedom am I being offered when I may be arrested on a pass offence? What freedom am I being offered to live my life as a family with my dear wife who remains in banishment in Brandfort? What freedom am I being offered when I must ask for permission to live in an urban area? What freedom am I being offered when I need a stamp in my pass to seek work? What freedom am I being offered when my very South African citizenship is not respected?

"Only free men can negotiate. Prisoners cannot enter into contracts.... I cannot and will not give any undertaking at a time when I and you, the people, are not free. Your freedom and mine cannot be separated. I will return."

South African government officials continued talks with Nelson Mandela over the next four years. In early 1989 Mandela wrote to Botha: "The deepening political crisis in our country has been a matter of grave concern to me for quite some time, and I now consider it necessary ... for the African National Congress and the government to meet urgently to negotiate an effective political settlement." The stalemate, however, continued until late 1989.

In October, F. W. de Klerk was elected state president of South Africa. He had run for office on a platform that promised negotiations and a peaceful resolution to the country's crisis. Many in South Africa and in the international community favoured this approach. De Klerk presented a plan for a new constitution. Although he said he did not believe in integration, he did believe in accepting the inevitability of a multiracial state.

That same month, Walter Sisulu and seven other prisoners from the Rivonia Trial[1] were released unconditionally.

In December, Mandela and de Klerk met and talked in Cape Town, at the president's office.

In early February 1990, de Klerk made several stunning announcements.

- *The African National Congress and 60 other organizations would be allowed to operate legally.*
- *Restrictions on 374 people would be lifted.*
- *There would be a temporary halt to executions.*

• The national state of emergency would soon be lifted.

• The government was committed to implementing a new constitution with no domination.

And, finally, the long-awaited announcement that the government would be releasing Mandela within days:

I am now in a position to announce that Mr. Nelson Mandela will be released at Victor Verster Prison.... We would all like Mr. Mandela's release to take place in a dignified and orderly manner.

The news conference announcing that Mandela would be released was seen live throughout the world.

At 4:15 p.m., Sunday, February 11, 1990, Nelson Mandela was released from prison for the first time in 10 000 days. He was 71 years old.

Epilogue

Millions around the world heard Mandela address the 50 000 people gathered in front of the Cape Town City Hall.

"AMANDLA!" Mandela chanted the Zulu word for power.

"NGAWETHU! It is ours," the crowd responded.

This had long been the chant of the black

resistance movement in South Africa.

"We have waited too long for freedom. We can wait no longer." The struggle, he urged, must continue on all fronts. There was no room for relaxing the pressures on the apartheid government.

He concluded the 20-minute speech with his own words, spoken at the Rivonia Trial—words, he said, that were as true today as they were a quarter century before.

> *I have fought against white domination, and I have fought against black domination. I have cherished the ideal of a democratic and free society in which all persons live together in harmony and with equal opportunities. It is an ideal which I hope to live for and to achieve. But if needs be, it is an ideal for which I am prepared to die.*

1. **Rivonia Trial**: The trial where Mandela and eight others were convicted of planning the overthrow of the government in 1964.

ACKNOWLEDGEMENTS

Permission to reprint copyright material is gratefully acknowledged. Every reasonable effort to trace the copyright holders of materials appearing in this book has been made. Information that will enable the publisher to rectify any error or omission will be welcomed.

"I never realized..." quotation from unknown title by Stephen Leacock. Used by permission of the Canadian Publishers, McClelland & Stewart, Toronto. **The Far Side** by Gary Larson © 1988 FarWorks Inc. Dist. by Universal Press Syndicate. Reprinted with permission. All rights reserved. **Belinda Enriquez, Period 3, Room 122** from *Back to Class* by Mel Glenn. Text copyright © 1988 by Mel Glenn. Reprinted by permission of Clarion Books/Houghton Mifflin Co. All rights reserved. **When did Human Beings Begin?** (original title "A Difficult Question") by Bruce Coville from *Prehistoric People* by Bruce Coville & Michael McDermott, Ill. Copyright © 1990 by Bruce Coville. Used by permission of Doubleday, a division of Bantam Doubleday Dell Publishing Group, Inc. **Wheels Make the World Go Round** (original title "Wheels within wheels") from Reader's Digest *Quest for the Past*. Copyright © 1984 The Reader's Digest Association, Inc. Reprinted by permission. **B.C. cartoon** by Johnny Hart reprinted by permission of Johnny Hart and Creators Syndicate, Inc. **The Egyptians Prepare for Life After Death** by Catherine Chadefaud from *The First Empires* © 1988 English text Silver Burdett Press. Used by permission. **The Greeks Explore Ideas** by Sophia A. Boyer and Winifred Lubell from *Gifts from the Greeks, Alpha to Omega,* copyright © 1970 by Sophia A. Boyer and Winifred Lubell. All rights reserved by the authors. **Hannibal Crosses the Alps with Elephants** (original title "Death in the Alps") from Reader's Digest *Quest for the Past*. Copyright © 1984 The Reader's Digest Association, Inc. Reprinted by permission. **Women Make Their Mark: Trung Trac and Trung Nhi** and **Jingo Kogo** from *The Encyclopedia of Amazons: Women Warriors from Antiquity to the Modern Era* by Jessica Amanda Salmonson, published by Paragon House, New York. Copyright © 1991 by Jessica Amanda Salmonson. Used by permission of Paragon House. **Elizabeth I** from *Collins Illustrated Encyclopedia of Famous*

People. Copyright © 1991 by Harper Collins. Copyright © 1991 Kenneth and Valerie McLeish. Reprinted by permission of HarperCollins Publishers Limited, London. **Catherine II ("The Great")** from *Great Lives* by Simon Boughton. Copyright © 1988 by Grisewood and Dempsey Ltd. Used by permission of Doubleday, a division of Bantam Doubleday Dell Publishing Group, Inc. **Vesuvius Erupts, Destroying Pompeii** by Catherine George reprinted with permission – The Toronto Star Syndicate. Originally titled "Beneath the Ashes" in the February 27, 1993, issue of *The Toronto Star*. **Eyewitness account by Pliny the Younger**, approx. 400 words (pp 171-172) from *The Letters of the Younger Pliny* translated by Betty Radice (Penguin Classics, 1963) copyright © Betty Radice, 1963, 1969. Reproduced by permission of Penguin Books Ltd. **The Vikings Sail to Newfoundland** by Suzanne LeVert from *Let's Discover Canada—Newfoundland*, pp. 17–20, by Suzanne LeVert; George Sheppard, General Editor. Copyright © 1992 by Chelsea House Publishers, a division of Main Line Book Co. Used by permission of Chelsea House Publishers. **Marco Polo Meets the Great Kublai Khan** (original title "Marco Polo and the Great Khan") by Kim Dramer from *World Leaders—Past & Present: Kublai Khan* volume, pp. 71-81. Copyright © 1990 by Chelsea House Publishers, a division of Main Line Book Co. Used by permission of Chelsea House Publishers. **Muhammad ibn-Batuta Travels the World** by William Scheller from *The World's Greatest Explorers*. Copyright © 1992 by The Oliver Press, Inc. Minneapolis. Used with permission. **The Black Death Changes Europe** (original title "The Black Death") from Reader's Digest *Quest for the Past*. Copyright © 1984 The Reader's Digest Association, Inc. Reprinted by permission. **Five Terrible Epidemics** excerpted from *The Kids' World Almanac of History*, by Deborah G. Felder, copyright © 1991 Deborah G. Felder. Reprinted with the permission of Funk & Wagnalls Corporation. The World Almanac is a registered trademark of Funk & Wagnalls Corporation. **Joan of Arc Fights for France** (original title "The Maid of Orléans") from *Great Lives* by Simon Boughton. Copyright © 1988 by Grisewood and Dempsey Ltd. Used by permission of Doubleday, a division of Bantam Doubleday Dell Publishing Group, Inc. **Moctezuma Rules the Aztecs** by Frances. F. Berdan, originally titled "The Aztecs," from *FACES'* June, 1990 issue: *Ancient Mexico*, © 1990,

Cobblestone Publishing, Inc., 7 School St., Peterborough, NH 03458 (except title and minor changes). Reprinted by permission of the publisher. **Taj Mahal, A Love Poem in Marble** by Leah Eskin from *Scholastic Update*, March 10, 1989 issue. **Britain and France Battle for Canada** by Karen Ford, Janet MacLean, and Barry Wansbrough from *Great Canadian Lives: Portraits in Heroism to 1867*. Copyright © 1985 by Nelson Canada, A Division of Thomson Canada Limited. **Australia: A Prison Colony Becomes a Nation** by Bob Black, originally titled "The Unknown Southern Land," from *FACES'* May, 1992 issue: *Australia Through Time*, © 1992, Cobblestone Publishing, Inc., 7 School St., Peterborough, NH 03458 (except for title and minor changes). Reprinted by permission of the publisher. **The Winds of Revolution** (original titles "American independence is declared," "Parisian mob storms the Bastille," "Bolsheviks stage bloodless coup") from *Chronicle of the World*, published in 1989 by Chronicle Communications Ltd., London. Copyright © 1989 Jacques Legrand S.A. International Publishing, Paris, for World English rights. **Simon Bolívar Dreams of South American Liberation** (original title "Simon Bolívar") by Kenneth and Valerie McLeish from *Collins Illustrated Encyclopedia of Famous People*. Copyright © 1991 by Harper Collins. Copyright © 1991 Kenneth and Valerie McLeish. Reprinted by permission of HarperCollins Publishers Limited, London. **African-Americans Fight to Abolish Slavery** by Howard Smead from *The Afro-Americans*, "American Slave Revolts" on pp. 42–47. Copyright © 1989 by Chelsea House Publishers, a division of Main Line Book Co. Used by permission of Chelsea House Publishers. **"Granma used to tell this story..."** by Betty Jones (originally from "The Negro in Virginia," p. 209, in "American Negro: His History & Literature," Ser. No. 2, 1969, reprint of 1940 edition), reprinted with permission from Ayer Company Publishers. **checking out me history** by John Agard from *Life Doesn't Frighten Me at All* compiled by John Agard, published by William Heinemann Ltd. Reprinted by permission. **Sitting Bull Triumphs at Little Bighorn** (original titles "Sitting Bull" and "Custer, George Armstrong") by Kenneth and Valerie McLeish from *Collins Illustrated Encyclopedia of Famous People*. Copyright © 1991 by Harper Collins. Copyright © 1991 Kenneth and Valerie McLeish. Reprinted by permission of HarperCollins Publishers Limited, London. **Campaigners for Women's**

Rights: Susan Brownell Anthony from *Great Lives* by Simon Boughton. Copyright © 1988 by Grisewood & Dempsey Ltd. Used by permission of Doubleday, a division of Bantam Doubleday Dell Publishing Group, Inc. **Emily Murphy** by Janet Lunn and Christopher Moore from *The Story of Canada* by Janet Lunn and Christopher Moore. Published by Lester Publishing/Key Porter Books. Used with permission. **How Two World Wars Began** (original titles "Archduke's murder unsettles Europe," "Europe is again at war," "USA joins the Allies") from *Chronicle of the World*, published in 1989 by Chronicle Communications Ltd., London. Copyright © 1989 Jacques Legrand S.A. International Publishing, Paris, for World English rights. **Uprising in the Warsaw Ghetto** by R. Conrad Stein excerpted from *World at War: Warsaw Ghetto* by R. Conrad Stein. Copyright © 1985 by Childrens Press, (R) Inc. Used with permission. **An Atomic Bomb Targets Hiroshima** (original title "The Decision That Changed the World") by Michael O'Neal adapted from Chapter One of *President Truman and the Atomic Bomb*, a volume in the *Great Mysteries* series, published by Greenhaven Press, San Diego, California. Copyright © 1990 Greenhaven Press. Reprinted with permission. **Neil Armstrong Lands on the Moon** (original title "Man on the Moon") from *Great Lives* by Simon Boughton. Copyright © 1988 by Grisewood and Dempsey Ltd. Used by permission of Doubleday, a division of Bantam Doubleday Dell Publishing Group, Inc. **History of Space** (original title "The Space Age") from *1,000 Great Events Through the Ages* by Brenda Ralph Lewis, Philip Steele, and Lynne Williams. Copyright © The Hamlyn Publishing Group Limited 1988. Reprinted by permission of Hamlyn Publishing. **The Berlin Wall Crashes Down** (original title "The Meanings of the Wall, November 16, 1989") by Robert Darnton from *Berlin Journal 1989–1990*, copyright © 1991 by Robert Darnton, published by W.W. Norton & Company, Inc., New York. **Nelson Mandela is Released from Prison** by Barry Denenberg from *Nelson Mandela: No Easy Walk to Freedom* by Barry Denenberg. Copyright © 1991 by Barry Denenberg. Reprinted by permission of Scholastic Inc.

THE EDITORS

Christine McClymont was born in Scotland, but came to Canada at an early age. For many years, she has been compiling anthologies for Nelson Canada series such as *Networks, In Context,* and *Features*. Christine enjoys hiking and cross-country skiing, and is actively involved with the Toronto Chamber Society.

James Barry is Chairman of the English Department at Brebeuf College School, North York, Ontario. He is the editor of the poetry anthologies *Themes on the Journey, Departures, Side by Side,* and *Poetry Express*, as well as an annual student writing anthology, *Triple Bronze*. Besides teaching, his special interests are sports (especially hockey), music, and student writing.

Berenice Wood is presently an instructor in the Faculty of Education at the University of Victoria. She has been an English Department Head and Secondary English Coordinator, and was responsible for developing the current Language Arts-English provincial curriculum for the B.C. Ministry of Education. Her interests include gardening, writing, and all generations of *Star Trek*.